Christ

Wisd[om]

is a Path B[ook]
offering practical spirituality
to enrich everyday living

"Your word is a lamp to my feet
and a light to my path."
Psalm 119:105

To the people of St. Philip's Anglican Church
Victoria, B.C.
"I thank my God every time I remember you."
(Philippians 1:3)

Christ Wisdom

Spiritual Practice in the
Beatitudes and the Lord's Prayer

Christopher Page

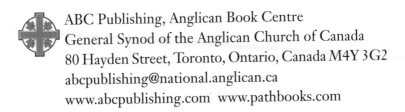

ABC Publishing, Anglican Book Centre
General Synod of the Anglican Church of Canada
80 Hayden Street, Toronto, Ontario, Canada M4Y 3G2
abcpublishing@national.anglican.ca
www.abcpublishing.com www.pathbooks.com

Text set in Janson
Cover and text design by Jane Thornton
Cover illustration: The Savior (6th-century Sinai icon), reprinted with permission from the web site of Dr. Alexander Boguslawski.

Library and Archives Canada Cataloguing in Publication
Page, Christopher, 1954-

Christ wisdom : spiritual practice in the Beatitudes and the Lord's Prayer / Christopher Page.

ISBN 1-55126-420-X

1. Jesus Christ—Teachings—Meditations.
2. Beatitudes—Meditations. 3. Lord's prayer—Meditations.
4. Spiritual life. I. Title.

BT382.P33 2004   242'.5   C2004-904272-6

Contents

Acknowledgements

"It takes a village to raise a child." It takes a community to create a book. Although the cover of this little book bears the name of a single author, it exists only because of the involvement of many people.

This book would not even have begun if it had not been for the people of St. Philip's Anglican Church. For sixteen years the people of this Christian community have shared with me in exploring and growing together in our journey towards the life of fullness in Christ. They have supported, challenged, and encouraged me in more ways than most of them will ever be aware. I cannot express strongly enough to them my deep gratitude and love.

The book would never have come into existence without the gentle prodding and bold initiative of Gillian Fosdick. She has been a constant source of strength, inspiration, challenge, and practical support in my life and in the ministry of St. Philip's Church.

The pages of this book bear witness to some of the writers and teachers who have shaped my spiritual life. Particularly, I am grateful to the teaching of Cynthia Bourgeault, who taught me the spiritual practice of Centering Prayer and set the direction of my spiritual life towards new depth.

I am also deeply grateful to the Diocese of British Columbia where I have been privileged to serve as a priest for the past sixteen years. The generosity of the Diocese and our Educational Trusts Board made possible a year's sabbatical study leave in 1998 to 1999. I continue to draw from the blessing of that gift in my ministry. A great deal of the value of that sabbatical year is thanks to the flexibility and guidance of the Vancouver School of Theology and particularly Donald Grayston and Gerald Hobbes.

Working on this book has brought me into contact with Robert Maclennan of ABC Publishing. I have been blessed by his gentle support and guidance in bringing this book to publication.

Finally, there are three women in my life who embody whatever Wisdom there may be in this book. I am filled with love and gratitude for my wife, Heather, who lives the Wisdom way of life with a depth, integrity, and beauty that are a source of endless inspiration and hope in my life. Our daughters, Rachel and Naomi, offer us the extraordinary gift of allowing us to see the Wisdom by which we hope to live carried in new vessels and lived in a new generation.

Unless otherwise noted, all biblical quotations are from *The New Revised Standard Version* of the Bible.

Introduction

As spiritual seekers we do not need more information about our faith. We need the tools of living transformed and transforming lives. These are the tools Jesus left to us hidden in the words of both the Beatitudes and the Lord's Prayer. These passages of Scripture are meant to be lived, not simply to be used as the basis for developing elaborate doctrines and theologies.

The words of Jesus are to be put into practice. They are intended to shape all the moments of our days in their most intimate details. These words exist to open us to a deeper dimension of reality in order that we may be empowered to live the lives for which we were created. They contain within them deep Wisdom for authentic human living.

Too often we settle for something much less than our true destiny as human beings. At the end of Matthew chapter 5 Jesus summed up his vision for human living saying, "Be perfect, therefore, as your heavenly Father is perfect" (Matthew 5:48). To be "perfect" is to be whole, complete. It is to live with integrity a life that is consistent because it flows in its entirety from a consistent place. To be perfect is to live with the deep Wisdom that is the gift of God. We cannot create this Wisdom for ourselves; we cannot manufacture it in our heads. It is a gift given to us by God's Holy Spirit through Jesus. We can prepare ourselves to receive the gift of Wisdom, but we are not the source of this gift.

Living with the Wisdom that these passages contain means living from a deep centred place within ourselves which is in communion with God. The Christian journey unfolds in our lives as we reconnect with our awareness of this centre and find

Christ at the heart of our heart. We were created to live with this Wisdom from the centre.

This centre is uncovered for us and is embodied in the life and teachings of Jesus. Jesus entered human history as the incarnation of God's loving Wisdom. Jesus' teaching has the power to convey to us that eternal Wisdom for living which is God's Spirit at work in the world. This Wisdom flows from a deep wellspring of life and truth to which Jesus bears witness at the centre of his being. The New Testament shows that, at the core of his life, Jesus lived in deep and intimate communion with God. Jesus' words and actions were always grounded in this inner awareness of his own divine nature.

We too can live from this centred place of Being. The teachings of the Christian faith are designed to reconnect us with the inner depths of our true humanness. Jesus' teaching aims to enable us to encounter life more fully and more authentically and to embrace all of life with greater Wisdom and compassion.

As we explore the Beatitudes, we will discover the central spiritual practices of the Christian faith. We will uncover the fundamental attitudes and gestures of faith that enable us to begin to embody Jesus' life-transforming vision. We cannot go away from a deep encounter with these teachings without being changed in profound ways.

Since the challenge to live in intimate communion with God lies at the heart of the Beatitudes, it makes sense to study along with the Beatitudes that other central piece of Jesus' teaching known as the Lord's Prayer. In the Lord's Prayer Jesus most fully reveals his heart and opens to us the way of deep intimate communion with God. This is the purpose of the human Creation. Our primary purpose in life is not to do good works or to measure up to some standard of behaviour, but to learn to rest in eternal communion with God and to live from that place of deep trust and faith.

The Beatitudes set out for us the attitudes and practices of the Christian life. The Lord's Prayer builds upon those principles and guides us in living in communion with God.

Too much of what passes today for Christian spirituality leads to greater fragmentation and brokenness within the human community. We need to discover new visions of Christian discipleship and uncover new ways of being in the world as followers of Jesus Christ. Jesus' teaching points us beyond the differences and dichotomies that divide so much of the Christian Church to the living of a common faith. He teaches spiritual practices with the power to bring us to the place where we understand that those things which unite us in the fellowship of God's children are greater than those things which divide us.

This book aims to look beyond the surface of life and to help us to see the deeper realities of life in the Spirit. It invites readers into a journey with Jesus that has the potential to open us to a deep inner wellspring of Wisdom and life.

Each chapter is followed by two sets of questions and then a practice exercise. The exercises are the heart of this book. They encourage us to pay close attention to our lives. They encourage us to stay close to that Wisdom that is our birthright in Christ. They have the potential to guide us to this place of Wisdom if we follow them faithfully and pay attention to the insights and understanding that they release in our lives.

By pondering the questions at the end of each chapter and following the exercises, we may discover new realms of being opening within ourselves. We may encounter the living Wisdom of God. We may find ourselves living from a new place. We may meet the world with fresh eyes and a renewed compassion and hope.

The Beatitudes

I

Life Beyond Circumstance

Matthew 5:1–2

When Jesus saw the crowds, he went up the mountain; and after he sat down, his disciples came to him. Then he began to speak, and taught them.

Mountains are important in the Bible. Moses went up a mountain to receive God's word for the Hebrew people. Joshua, Moses' successor, built an altar and renewed Israel's connection with God's law on a mountain. Elijah, the great prophet, encountered God on a mountain and received there God's instructions to anoint new kings for Israel and Judah.

So the mountain is the place of encounter with God. It is the place where you expect to hear from God and where you go to make an authoritative pronouncement on God's behalf.

Matthew tells us that when Jesus "saw the crowds, he went up the mountain; and after he sat down, his disciples came to him. Then he began to speak, and taught them." By going "up the mountain" Jesus is saying, "Pay close attention. The words that I am going to speak are important; they carry unique authority." When Jesus speaks from the mountain, we are intended to encounter God in this teaching and receive the illumination of God's presence.

The long teaching section that follows these two introductory verses, extending from Matthew chapter 5 through to the end of chapter 7, is known as The Sermon on the Mount. The mountain location from which these words are spoken alerts us to the fact that these words constitute the heart of Jesus' understanding of and teaching about the spiritual life.

Although biblical scholars wrestle and struggle over almost every piece of the New Testament, arguing about whether Jesus said this bit or did not say that bit, there is almost universal agreement that in the words of The Sermon on the Mount, we are coming as close as we can to the authentic, original voice of Jesus the Teacher.

Having taken his place of authoritative pronouncement, "Jesus began to speak, and taught them saying: Blessed...." The Sermon on the Mount begins with a series of aphorisms. A careful study of these short sayings ushers us into the spiritual environment that forms the basis for understanding the rest of Jesus' sermon and living it in our own lives.

Nine times between verses 3 and 11 in Matthew chapter 5, Jesus says *makarioi*. The word is translated most commonly as "blessed." So this section of Scripture has come to be known as the "Beatitudes" from the Latin word for "blessed."

"Blessed" is a good translation of the Greek word *makarioi*. But an equally good translation, perhaps even better for our purposes, would be the word "happy." In chapters 5, 6, and 7 of Matthew's gospel we have Jesus' gift to us, his prescription for living a happy, or blessed, or even blissful life.

Perhaps the word "happy" sounds trite to our sophisticated ears. But Jesus connects some strange things with his idea of happiness: "Happy are the poor in spirit... Happy are the ones who mourn... Happy are those who hunger and thirst... Happy are those who are persecuted... Happy are you when people revile you."

Five of the eight "happinesses" listed in Matthew 5:3–11 are connected with difficult things. If I were to offer you poverty, mourning, hunger, thirst, persecution, and reviling, you would not line up to receive my gifts. And yet these are some of the qualities that Jesus connects with his understanding of happiness.

Our problem with the concept of happiness is that we tend to think it depends on external circumstances. We think happiness means everything going nicely for us, like lying on a warm beach with the gentle sound of the ocean lapping at the shore.

However, right at the outset of his sermon, Jesus announces that he is introducing an entirely different concept of happiness, one that does not depend on external circumstances. Jesus is pointing the way to a happiness that comes from a deeper place.

The problem with external circumstances is that they are impermanent. They change. External circumstances that once seemed to be a source of happiness will eventually become a source of unhappiness.

I listen to a parent talk about her adult child who has become enormously successful in the corporate world. The external circumstances of this person's life should make anyone happy — success, power, wealth, prestige. Who could ask for anything more? But this mother speaks of her desperate concern for her successful son who is being eaten alive by his job.

Think of a young person desperate to find the right life partner, who will bring great joy and fulfillment. Finally a wonderful romance is born and blossoms into marriage. Over the years, the romance runs out and the relationship becomes a source of pain for husband and wife. The circumstance that once brought happiness now seems only to produce suffering.

In both cases, the very set of circumstances that at first brought happiness, fulfillment, self-esteem, and gratification turned into a monster that was destroying the life it had once seemed to nurture.

If we are to experience *makarioi*, we must find something that can transcend circumstances. We must find a way of living that goes beyond the seesaw ups and downs of pleasure and pain. The gift that Jesus offers is the spiritual skill for living life less dependent on circumstance and free of the inevitable ups and downs, twists and turns, of fickle fate. Jesus focuses our attention on the inner life and teaches us the skill of resting and trusting in him so that our lives become truly free.

1. What do our usual visions of happiness look like? What are the risks in our vision of happiness? How does Jesus' vision of happiness look different? Which version of happiness has the most weight and strength? Why?

2. What would a life free of endless ups and downs look like? Identify a person you know or have met who seems to live independently of external circumstance. What gives them this ability? What was this person's impact?

Watch for things in your life to which you look for a sense of happiness. Ask yourself what would happen if your life changed and you were no longer able to have this thing or person or situation in your life, which had once made you happy. Feel within yourself the possibility of a deeper source of happiness.

2

The Path
of Poverty

Matthew 5:3

Blessed are the poor in spirit, for theirs is the kingdom of
heaven.

Luke's version of the first Beatitude says, "Blessed are the poor,
for theirs is the kingdom of God."

Matthew and Luke use the same word for *poor*. Luke uses it
in a number of places, and whenever he does, it always means
"poor people" — those who do not have enough material pro-
vision to support their lives. Other than in this first Beatitude,
Matthew uses the word in only one other place, a discussion
about costly ointment and how it could have been sold and the
money given to "the poor" (Matthew 26). Once again "the poor"
are clearly people in material need.

This first Beatitude, especially in Luke's version, may seem
at best ridiculous, at worst offensive. Jesus seems to be saying,
"Happy are poor people." But we know that material poverty
is no guarantee of happiness. An overdraft at the bank and a
stack of unpaid bills do not bring anyone into a state of bliss. It

is possible to be miserable in poverty every bit as much as it is possible to be miserable with great wealth. Getting rid of all your possessions and going to live in a homeless shelter will not get you any closer to God or any closer to being happy than winning a million dollars in the lottery and retiring to a beach in Bermuda.

Matthew's version of this Beatitude adds to "poor" the qualifying phrase "in spirit," making it clear that Jesus is not referring to an external condition but to an inner attitude. For Matthew, the poverty Jesus speaks about is a spiritual condition, not a function of socio-economic status.

We need to be careful, however, not to move too quickly away from the literal meaning of the Greek word "poor." There can be a benefit in material poverty to the person who allows it to work internally.

So what is the potential gift in poverty? Poverty has the capacity to help us see through the illusion of external things. People who are poor have the opportunity to learn that external things cannot satisfy the deepest longings of our lives.

Rich people can hang on longer to the illusion that there is satisfaction to be found on the surface of life. This is why Jesus said, "It will be hard for a rich person to enter the kingdom of heaven" (Matthew 19:23). It is more difficult for the rich to recognize how deeply impoverished they actually are. When our lives are filled with accomplishments, toys, distractions, and talents, we never have to face the reality of our own emptiness and need.

And the only thing that prevents any of us from knowing the presence of God in our lives is the refusal to recognize our need. As long as we believe that we can make our lives work on our own, we will never find God. The blessing of poverty is that it has the power to show us that we cannot make our lives work by our own clever plans and devices.

Christianity is not a self-help program; it is a self-surrender program. The stronger, more powerful, more talented, and more in control we are, the more difficult it is for us to surrender. The more we have to let go of, the more difficult it is to let go.

The Sermon on the Mount is trying to make us recognize that true life is lived in an entirely different realm than that of that we are normally most conscious. We are not truly alive until we recognize that there is a deeper inner reality to life which cannot come alive within us until we acknowledge the insufficiency of everything on the surface.

One of the most profound and beautiful things Thomas Merton ever wrote was in his early book *The Sign of Jonas*:

> Every creature that enters my life, every instant of my days, will be designed to wound me with the realization of the world's insufficiency, until I become so detached that I will be able to find God alone in everything. Only then will all things bring me joy.[1]

This is the reason Jesus connects poverty to happiness. Poverty has the power to open our eyes to "the world's insufficiency" and to the possibility of discovering our true humanity in a totally different dimension of reality.

Jesus calls this new dimension "the kingdom of heaven. Blessed are the poor in spirit, for theirs is the kingdom of heaven." Notice this is not future tense. Jesus does not hold out the promise of the kingdom like a carrot dangled in front of your face. Nor is Jesus saying that it is good to put up with poverty for now because later you will get your reward in heaven. Instead, The Sermon on the Mount opens a whole new dimension of reality in which it is possible to live a fulfilled, deep, meaningful, rich life now, regardless of our external circumstances.

---

1. Thomas Merton, *The Sign of Jonas* (New York: Harcourt Brace Jovanovich, 1953), p. 51.

Those who face their inner poverty can be transported into this new dimension. Having surrendered the hopeless task of trying to make their lives work on their own, they discover a new place of being where God is the only reality, a place in which we are "able to find God alone in everything." Then everything can bring us joy.

In this new realm we know that all the things we worry over are just on the surface of life. They do not trouble us in the deeper realm of the human spirit, our life in God. We can only come to this awareness through the recognition of our own poverty and the absolute poverty of everything outside of God.

Jesus is not calling us to get stuck in our poverty or to make a new identity out of it. The gift of our poverty is to move us beyond poverty into a new spiritual realm in which we find that God alone can satisfy our lives.

The cross of Christ is the ultimate sign of human poverty. It was poverty of human spirit which caused Jesus to be betrayed, condemned, and crucified, just as poverty of human spirit destroys the peace of our human community. But by embracing the poverty of the cross, Jesus showed a new way. Jesus opened the gates to a new dimension of life in which all our poverty is transformed into the glory of resurrection. Through the cross we can discover that indeed, "Blessed are the poor in spirit, for theirs is the kingdom of heaven."

1. What is your vision of richness? What illusion is offered by material prosperity, talents, and accomplishments? What does it take for us to get over our belief in this illusion?

2. What does it feel like to stop running from our own poverty? What change takes place when we are willing to see and accept our poverty?

Look at the busyness and the intensity of the world around you. Step aside for a moment from all that activity, determination, pressure, and striving. See it as a game being played out on the surface of life. Recognize that there is a deeper reality within that is more real and more life-giving than all that surface activity.

3

The Lesson of Mourning

Blessed are those who mourn, for they will be comforted.

Of the nine prescriptions for happiness that Jesus offers in the Beatitudes, number two is almost certainly one of the oddest: "Happy are those who mourn," or more literally, "Happy are the mourning ones." Unfortunately there is no way to slip out of the oddity by changing the translation. The word translated as mourn is *pentheo* and it means "be sad, grieve, or mourn."

Neither will the grammar of this verse allow us to solve the puzzle of happy mourning ones by merely putting the happiness off into some later period. Jesus does not say, "Happy *will* be the mourning ones when they stop mourning." He says, "Blessed are those who mourn." It is almost as if he is saying, "Happy are those who are unhappy."

So what kind of mourning or unhappiness makes an unhappy person happy in the very midst of their unhappiness?

The Greek word *pentheo* occurs only three times in the gospels, once here and once in Luke's shorter version of the

Beatitudes. The only other place it occurs is in Matthew 9:15 where John the Baptist's disciples ask Jesus why his disciples do not fast. Jesus replies saying, "The wedding guests cannot pentheo as long as the bridegroom is with them, can they? The days will come when the bridegroom is taken away from them, and then they will fast." So fasting is a sign of *pentheo*, and *pentheo* is in response to the absence of the bridegroom. The bridegroom is Jesus. So, Jesus is saying that the disciples will mourn when he is absent.

But there is a twist in this statement in Matthew 9:15. When we read about the absent bridegroom, we need to remember that at the end of Matthew's gospel, Jesus says, "Remember, I am with you always, to the end of the age" (Matthew 28:20). The fact is that the bridegroom is never missing.

So, if mourning is connected to the absence of Jesus and Jesus is never absent, does this mean that we never need to mourn and the second Beatitude has no place in our lives?

I don't think so. Notice that Jesus says, "Remember, I am with you always." We are to *remember*. Our problem is that we forget that Jesus is with us always, and when we forget, we mourn. All our mourning arises out of a sense of the absence of God.

We think we are sad about things going wrong in our lives — a broken relationship, not getting on at work, our ambitions unrealized, our talents unused, our aspirations frustrated. We focus on the pain, the uncertainty, and the fear that are inevitable in life and feel that we are alone in an unfriendly and hostile universe. But actually our misery comes from allowing external things to cause us to forget.

We forget that there is an abundant source of life and love dwelling within us. We forget that, in fact, life is stronger than death. We forget that the violence of the cross could not destroy the Prince of Peace. And when we forget, we mourn.

The purpose of mourning is to wake us up to what we have forgotten. The sadness and dissatisfaction in our lives should alert us to noticing that we have attached ourselves to something in the hope that it might make us happy. Mourning is a guide, directing us to recognize that we have become overly attached to something other than God. This recognition makes it possible for us to let go of our attachment and return to that place of depth in which lies the only hope of human happiness.

Rowan Williams points out something from the teaching of John of the Cross: "Growth in spiritual maturity is growth in detachment from the creaturely."[1] This is not a denial of the value of Creation. It is simply putting all external reality into proper perspective, recognizing that human beings were created for a destiny greater than attachment to "the creaturely."

It is important to keep in mind that Jesus does not say, "Blessed are those who whine." Whining demonstrates our belief that happiness depends on our external circumstances being the way we would like them to be. When I whine, I am hoping someone will rescue me and fix my life.

Mourning accepts that there is no way to fix all the external brokenness of life. The mourning that Jesus is talking about is a signpost calling us to see that we have been looking in the wrong places. We have been trying to meet a need in a way that the need can never be met. We have been trying to quench our thirst with salt water.

The good news is that, as soon as we see this in ourselves, we also see that the thing for which we truly long has already been given. "Remember, I am with you always." So the mourning becomes the source of comfort. "Blessed are those who mourn, for they will be comforted."

---

1   Rowan Williams, *The Wound of Knowledge: Christian Spirituality from the New Testament to St. John of the Cross* (London: Darton, Longman and Todd, 1979), p. 163.

The word "comforted" here is important. The Greek word is *parakaleo*. It is the same root word that appears in John's gospel where Jesus is reported to have said to his disciples,

> If you love me, you will keep my commandments. And I will ask the Father, and he will give you another *parakaleo* to be with you forever. This is the Spirit of truth, whom the world cannot receive, because it neither sees him nor knows him. You know him, because he abides with you, and he will be in you (John 14:15–17).

To find what you long for you need only look within. What you seek abides with you and is in you. You don't need to wait until you get everything in life sorted out in order to know that the comfort for which you long has been given. You need only to remember. You need only to let those hints of sadness and discomfort wake you up to reality. You are not alone. The Holy Spirit of God, the vitality and power of the universe, lives within your deepest inner being. Everything for which you have ever longed is given by God, through Christ, in the Holy Spirit.

Thomas Merton says,

> We have found Him, He has found us. We are in Him, He is in us. There is nothing further to look for, except for the deepening of this life we already possess. Be content.[2]

You don't need a new toy or a holiday to fill the empty space in your life. Even a new job or job security, a new relationship or

---

2 Thomas Merton, *A Search for Solitude: The Journals of Thomas Merton volume three 1952–1960* (San Francisco: Harper Collins, 1996), p. 70.

your children's success, will not make everything turn out alright.

Your mourning can wake you up to your true longing, which is for God. God already lives at the centre of your being. The moment you open your eyes to see, you discover God's face smiling at the heart of your heart, embracing your need and loving you as you are.

1. What do we believe are the real causes of unhappiness in life? What makes human beings so often seem to be drawn to things that make them unhappy?

2. What positive function can mourning play in our lives? How have you experienced this in your own life? Where did you expect to find comfort in the midst of your mourning?

When you experience mourning, try to identify that thing outside of yourself to which you have become attached and which is feeling threatened. Feel the change when you loosen your grip on this thing and let it go.

4

Gentle People

Matthew 5:5

Blessed are the meek, for they will inherit the earth.

In his little poem, "A Warning To My Readers," the Kentucky poet Wendell Berry offers a suitable preface to any discussion of this beatitude:

Do not think me gentle
because I speak in praise
of gentleness, or elegant
because I honor the grace
that keeps this world. I am
a man crude as any,
gross of speech, intolerant,
stubborn, angry, full
of fits and furies. That I
may have spoken well
at times, is not natural.
A wonder is what it is.[1]

---

1   Wendell Berry, *Collected Poems 1957–1982* (New York: North Point Press, 1984), p. 213.

Beatitude number three is enormously challenging: "Blessed are the meek, for they will inherit the earth." It is even more challenging if the word for *meek* is translated as "gentle" as in the *New American Standard Bible*, the *Jerusalem Bible*, and the *New English Bible*: "Blessed are the gentle, for they shall inherit the earth."

Gentle is a beautiful word. The same Greek word appears later in 1 Peter 3:4. Here for some reason the NRSV translators abandon their use of the word "meek" and translate the Greek word with the English word "gentle." So Peter writes, "Let your adornment be the inner self with the lasting beauty of a gentle and quiet spirit." True beauty lies within, and it is shown by a gentle and quiet spirit.

I am not sure that a gentle and quiet spirit is ever going to be a wildly popular life goal for most people. Most of us tend to be more drawn towards qualities like high energy, high achievement, and obvious competence.

We probably fail to value gentleness because we fail to understand its true nature. Few of us would associate gentleness with the promise Jesus attaches to it in the Beatitudes: "Blessed are the gentle, for they will inherit (or take possession of) the earth." Not many of us would think that gentle people are the ones most likely to take possession of the earth. Our usual model of leadership is based on a take-charge vision. We want leaders who are in control and can "kick butt" when necessary. We look for leaders who are aggressive and have high energy and iron self-discipline. Gentle people are seldom put in charge of things.

Our problem with this Beatitude is it does not seem practical. We believe that we need to look after ourselves, take charge, get life under control. If we don't go out there and get things going, life will pass us by and we will be walked over and left in the dust. Richard Rohr describes our condition this way:

We are culturally taught that everything out there is hostile. I have to compare, dominate, control, and insure. In brief, I have to be in charge. That need to be in charge moves us deeper and deeper into a world of anxiety.[2]

"That need to be in charge" moves us far from the world of gentleness. It is hard to be gentle when you are responsible for running the show or when you have to look out for yourself all the time and keep your guard up. Gentleness does not work well in a world of anxiety and fear where everyone is fighting desperately for his or her little piece of a pie that feels far too small.

The promise that the gentle will inherit the earth is repeated by Jesus in a slightly different form at the end of Matthew 6:31–33. Here Jesus is discussing the anxiety and fear which work against gentleness:

> Therefore do not worry, saying, "What will we eat?" or "What will we drink?" or "What will we wear?" for it is the Gentiles who strive for all these things; and indeed your heavenly Father knows that you need all these things. But strive first for the kingdom of God and his righteousness, and all these things will be given to you as well.

"Inherit the earth" is simply another way of saying, "You will have everything you need." So this Beatitude is saying, "Blessed are the gentle, for they find what they need."

You have probably heard the saying, "God helps those who help themselves." This particular piece of folk wisdom is not in

---

2 Richard Rohr, *Everything Belongs: The Gift of Contemplative Prayer* (New York: Crossroad Publishing, 1999), p. 61.

the Bible. In fact, Jesus' teaching suggests that the only ones God cannot look after are the ones who are determined to look after themselves. God can only look after us when we have finally accepted that we are actually incapable of looking after ourselves. That is why "Blessed are the poor in spirit... Blessed are those who mourn... and Blessed are the gentle." Blessed are those who have come to the end of their human resources and have realized that the deeper inner things for which their hearts truly long can only be given by the grace of God.

We may be able to do a reasonable job of building a great career, having a lovely family, making lots of money, being successful and powerful. The problem is that these small goals will eventually let us down. The career will end in retirement or lay off. The family will become a source of pain. The money will run out or someone will have more. We will eventually discover that we cannot inherit the earth by our own power.

By contrast, inheriting the earth means being fed and nourished in the depths of our being so that we can be sustained even when external things let us down.

It is the gentle people who are sustained because they are willing to let go. Having come to the end of striving, grasping, demanding, needing, craving, and longing, they have learned to trust and to live in response to the inner prompting of God's Spirit. Gentle people know that God is the only force capable of bringing true goodness into this world.

An inheritance is given as a gift. We do not build our inheritance or receive it through any merit of our own. It is given simply by virtue of our relationship. Gentle people know that they are related to God as children to a parent. Gentle people are open to receiving the inheritance of life. That is why they can afford to be gentle. Moving gently through life, they may appear to make less impact, but their power comes from being inwardly transformed. Having given up fighting for things that they then have to protect, they are courageous because they know that the inner Christ is their protection.

Gentle people are free with a freedom that can only come from the Christ who lives within us.

1. What does gentleness look like? Where have you seen gentleness at work? What did it look like? What impact does gentleness have in the world?

2. What attitude is most likely to hinder our openness to God's work in our lives? What causes such an attitude? What might we do to free God to be more fully at work in our lives?

Feel the difference within yourself between a hard response and a gentle response. Become conscious of the tendency towards subtle violence in yourself and in the world around you. Try a more gentle response in situations where you are tempted to respond with aggression, control, determination, and resistance.

5

What Are You Hungry For?

Matthew 5:6

Blessed are those who hunger and thirst for righteousness, for they will be filled.

There are many versions of the legend of the baby eagle who became separated from his family and was adopted and raised by barnyard chickens. The eagle grew into a mighty bird among the chickens, but unaware of his true nature, he continued to scratch and scrabble in the dirt among what he thought were his fellow chickens. It was only when a great adult eagle spied this young eagle from the sky and swooped down to teach him his true destiny that he discovered his natural identity and finally soared as the eagle he really was.

In the Christian faith, Jesus is the great adult eagle who swooped down from heavenly realms to reveal our true identity and to teach us to live according to our full destiny. Most often Jesus taught us our true identity simply by living it, but he also taught using words. One of the places Jesus taught the true nature of human identity most clearly is in the Beatitudes.

Of all the Beatitudes that show us our true nature, the one that perhaps gives us the clearest picture of who we really are is "Blessed are those who hunger and thirst after righteousness, for they shall be filled."

The Bible is full of stories and images of food. Like all living things, we must eat and drink in order to survive. Built into us is a mechanism that automatically signals when our body is in need of nourishment. If we ignore these signals for too long, we will become sick, and if we continue to ignore the wisdom of our bodies, we will eventually die of starvation or dehydration. When we hear Jesus say, "Blessed are those who hunger and thirst," we are intended to recognize that this Beatitude is addressed to all human beings because we all hunger and thirst.

But we probably do not all experience our hunger and thirst as a blessing. In fact, being hungry and thirsty can be a source of irritation, unpleasantness, and even danger. Jesus is obviously not saying that every kind of hunger and thirst is a source of blessing. Blessing comes from a particular kind of hunger and thirst: "Blessed are those who hunger and thirst for righteousness."

What is this righteousness that brings blessing to those who hunger and thirst for it? The word translated "righteousness" appears 92 times in the New Testament. Of those 92 occurrences, 36 are in Paul's letter to the Romans. The first time Paul uses the word in Romans is in 1:16–17a.

> For I am not ashamed of the gospel; it is the power of God for salvation to everyone who has faith, to the Jew first and also to the Greek. For in it the righteousness of God is revealed through faith.

The gospel which Paul proclaimed is the news of God in Jesus Christ. For Paul, Christ reveals the true nature of God. So the word "righteousness" stands for the nature and the person of God. To hunger and thirst for righteousness is to desire God.

In the spring of 1977 at the age of twenty-two, I graduated from the University of Victoria. As soon as I finished my last exam, I packed my bags, stepped on an airplane, and flew to the Yukon, where I spent four months working in a mining camp as I had done for two other summers during my undergraduate studies. But the summer of '77 was different because, three days after my return to Victoria, I was to be married. It was the longest summer of my life, spent longing, pining, hungering, and thirsting for my beloved. This was before email and I rarely had access to a telephone. The only way to communicate was by snail mail. The desire for the presence of the woman I was going to marry was like the hunger and thirst for righteousness that Jesus names: "Blessed are those who long to know God's presence."

No one had to tell me to hunger and thirst for my fiancée. It did not require self-discipline to long for her. My desire was a natural expression of my being. Similarly, to hunger and thirst for righteousness is our true human condition. Just as it is natural to long for food and water or for a fiancée from whom one is separated, so it is natural for us to long for God.

The sad reality, however, is that we often forget what it is we are really hungry and thirsty for. We forget that our true longing is for God. So we fill our lives with other things to avoid facing the hunger in the deepest part of our being. It is as if I had spent my summer dating every girl I could find instead of writing long passionate love letters to my beloved far away in Victoria. Those other girls could not satisfy the longing of my heart.

Because my hunger and thirst were focused in what for me was the right place, they became a blessing. The central challenge of the Beatitudes is to recognize what it is we really long for. Then the longing can be satisfied: "Blessed are those who hunger and thirst for righteousness, for they will be filled."

We do not have to work at being hungry and thirsty or at

being filled. We do need to ensure that our hunger and thirst are focused in the right place. When you are filling up on potato chips, there is no room for broccoli. Junk food has a certain intensity of flavour and immediate, if short term, gratification, but it lacks real nourishment.

When I think back to the years of courtship leading up to my marriage, I have to admit that things have changed a little in my relationship with that young woman I married in the summer of 1977. I confess there is not quite the same intensity of feeling and romance in our relationship today as there was then. But twenty-five years later romance has been replaced by something much deeper, more lasting, more real — something more like the fullness of God that comes to those who hunger and thirst for righteousness.

There is a deep abiding steadiness in my relationship with my wife, which is the closest parallel I know in earthly terms to the fullness God gives to those who hunger and thirst for righteousness. It is a steadiness that does not rise and fall on the fickle whims of feeling and that cannot be diminished by an occasional disagreement or dispute. It is a fullness that runs deeper than passing fancy or the intensity of romance. In it is the fullness of love that comes from God. It reflects the abiding presence of God who never lets you down.

We need to examine the junk food in our lives and give ourselves the opportunity to feast at the table of God's righteousness. Then we will be truly filled with all good things. Then we will soar like the eagle we were created to be.

1. What are the primary hungers that we experience? Where are those hungers directing us? What do our hungers indicate about the true nature of the human condition?

2. How have you experienced the fullness that Jesus promises will come to those who hunger and thirst for righteousness? What does this fullness feel like?

Next time you experience a sense of longing and desire for something, identify the object to which it is attached. See if you can hold that attachment more lightly and find a deeper inner fullness.

6

Giving and Receiving Mercy

Matthew 5:7

Blessed are the merciful, for they will receive mercy.

If the heart of the universe is the steady beat of God's mercy, why do so many of us seem to spend so much of our lives in a state of frenzied unrest? The answer to this troubling question lies in Jesus' Beatitude of mercy: "Blessed are the merciful, for they will receive mercy."

As with the petition in the Lord's Prayer where we are instructed to pray, "Forgive us our debts as we forgive our debtors," Jesus seems to be saying here that the universe is ordered in such a way that we will get what we give.

It is a foundational principle of the spiritual journey that we get back from life what we put into life. If we are always pouring forth frantic, grasping, needy, intense, dramatic energy into the world, this is exactly what we will receive back. If we release steady, *merciful*, peaceful, grounded energy into the world, this is what we will receive in return.

The word "mercy" has a rich, deep heritage upon which

Jesus drew when he said, "Blessed are the merciful, for they will receive mercy." The Hebrew Scriptures are full of mercy, particularly God's. My favourite example of the use of the word is in the gloomy book of Lamentations where the prophet is complaining, one might even say whining, to God about the sad state of his life:

> The thought of my affliction and my homelessness is wormwood and gall! My soul continually thinks of it and is bowed down within me (Lamentations 3:19–20).

Then suddenly in the midst of his mourning, the prophet's heart turns. He goes on to say:

> But this I call to mind, and therefore I have hope:The steadfast love of the Lord never ceases; his mercies never come to an end; they are new every morning; great is your faithfulness (Lamentations 3:21–3).

Mercy is the quality of God's steadfast, unchangeable love, which never gives up, never lets go. Mercy contains compassion, faithfulness, tenderness, understanding, kindness, and goodness towards the object of its love.

At the core of existence this divine quality of mercy is found. It is at the heart of God that beats and beats and beats with unconditional love. It never ceases, never changes, always forgives, always welcomes. It is the stability at the heart of the universe and at the centre of human life. God promises mercy to all people and never goes back upon this eternal covenant. God's mercy will not surrender to the changes and chances of outrageous fortune. You can trust God's mercy absolutely.

For many of us much of the time, this is not the way we experience life. Life does not always seem to be steady and reliable. More often it seems to be characterized by change, uncertainty, turmoil, upheaval, even chaos. We live frenetic, panicked lives, feeling as if we were driven obsessively by some wild out-of-control force that compels us to flit from one thing to another.

But at the heart of Jesus' teaching stands the principle of reciprocity: we get back from life what we put into it. According to this principle, we encounter in our panic more and more signs of the uncertainty and fragmentation of life. We become victims of a self-fulfilling prophecy in which darkness begets greater darkness until it becomes difficult for us to discern any light at all.

None of the Beatitudes is intended to beat us over the head with guilt in the vain hope of motivating us to live different lives. This one, like the others, is simply a description of reality. It reminds us that to some degree, we create our world from the inner state of our being. We draw to ourselves what we contain within ourselves. "Blessed are the merciful, for they will receive mercy."

If we want to experience life as filled with mercy, we must be merciful. If we want to know the steady, unchanging, compassionate strength of God, we must become people who are steady, unchanging, compassionate, and strong. Mercy draws mercy. You create for yourself what you give to others. The more insanity we put out there, the more insanity we get back. The more peaceful, quiet, steady force we generate, the more mercy we will experience in our own lives.

This is why the practice of silent, meditative prayer has become so important to so many people in their practice of the spiritual life. When we sit in silent prayer we are resting in the silent, loving mercy of God. By sitting still and doing nothing, we express our trust in God's mercy. We practice surrendering to God's mercy. At this point of stillness and quiet, we do not need to do anything, achieve anything. There is nothing to prove. We don't have to be good enough or strong enough. We simply accept the givenness of life.

In silent prayer we do not try to accomplish anything or to persuade God to do something for us or for the world. We are not trying to build even God's kingdom. For a few moments we are resting in the miracle of simply not trying. We are practicing letting go, and as we let go, we enter into the deep wellspring of God's mercy. We are at peace in that place, learning to trust the flow of God's mercy.

We cannot think our way to this state of rest. Good works will not get us there. Workshops, discussion groups, even Bible study, will not bring us to the land of transparent trust in the mercy of God. We get to this place of rest and trust only by resting and trusting.

Cynthia Bourgeault, speaking about the meditation practice known as Centering Prayer, says it "is a method based entirely on patterning into the subconscious the gesture of surrender."[1] Meditation is practice in letting go. Letting go enables us to grow in our ability to rest and trust in the awareness of being held by the mercy of God.

Since resting and trusting are not natural instincts for us, we have to create an environment in which we practice surrendering ourselves to God's faithful presence. The daily discipline of silent prayer is the environment in which trust can grow in our hearts. As we sit, we are exercising the muscles of surrender. And surrender is the only path to the place of trust at the centre of our being where we can experience the mercy of God.

This place of rest is not a place of escape or irresponsibility. It is, in fact, the only place from which balanced, sane action

---

1   Cynthia Bourgeault, *The Wisdom Way of Knowing: Reclaiming an Ancient Tradition to Awaken the Heart* (San Francisco: Jossey-Bass, 2003), p. 104.

can flow. From that place of trust, we can emerge to encounter the world in a new way. Bourgeault makes the point beautifully when she writes, "Interior surrender is often precisely what makes it possible to see a decisive action that must be taken and to do it with courage and strength. To ski down a hill or split a piece of wood, you first have to relax inwardly; only then can you exert the right force and timing."[2]

We come away from the silence carrying within us a deeper knowledge of God's mercy and prepared to go into the world to be merciful towards all Creation. Having rested in this place of absolute, unconditional acceptance and welcome, it becomes natural to live a more merciful life.

In Hebrew the word that is translated as "mercy" is closely related to the word "compassion." Mercy is the source of compassion. Resting in mercy means growing in compassion. True compassion is not a law we can follow; it is a way of being. So silent, meditative prayer is not an escape from reality. It is the only means I know of allowing us to encounter reality and find that it is fundamentally free, loving, and compassionate. And only when we are ready to meet life in an open, non-violent way can we be truly compassionate.

To be merciful is to be free to love in a way that does not bind or need or grasp or control. To be merciful is to have no agenda for another person. To be merciful is to be surrendered to the Merciful One. Then we will know that "Blessed are the merciful," and then we will discover the mercy that we have been enabled to give.

---

2 Ibid., p. 75.

1. What does mercy look like? What prevents us from experiencing mercy?

2. How might we grow in our ability to trust in God's mercy?

Explore a discipline of meditative prayer like Centering Prayer or Christian Meditation. Find a practice that works for you and follow it. Observe the impact this has upon your life.

7

The Heart
of the Matter

Matthew 5:8

Blessed are the pure in heart, for they will see God.

In all the Beatitudes, Jesus presents a condition and a promise. The condition in this one is purity of heart. The promise is seeing God: "Blessed are the pure in heart, for they will see God."

In Exodus 33:20 God says to Moses, "You cannot see my face; for no one shall see me and live." But as so often when we quote only one verse from one part of the Bible, we do not get the whole picture. Think of Job. At the end of his ordeal, Job says to God, "I had heard of you by the hearing of the ear, but now my eye sees you" (Job 42:5). Or think of the prophet Isaiah: "In the year that King Uzziah died, I saw the Lord sitting on a throne, high and lofty; and the hem of his robe filled the temple" (Isaiah 6:1). Here in the Beatitudes Jesus says, "Blessed are the pure in heart for they will see God."

In ordinary conversation we use the verb "to see" in a variety of ways. If you say to me, "I see that you keep your hair cut quite short," it is pretty clear that your eyes have been focussed on the top of my head. You might have all kinds of strange ideas about why I cut my hair so short. But if I explain that I keep my hair short simply because I don't like to fuss with it, you might reply saying, "Oh I see." In this second sense of "see," you would mean something like, "I understand," or "I perceive the reason." You would be talking about an inner process of perceiving.

Jesus uses the word "see" in this Beatitude in the second sense. In this sense God can be seen absolutely everywhere at all times. We are invited to perceive the presence of God in all life. We are invited to know, even to experience, that God is never absent from Creation or from our lives.

How do we come to this perception of the abiding presence of God? How are we going to see God? Jesus tells us we must be pure in heart.

What does it mean to be pure in heart? Let's start with the word "heart." In the Bible, the heart includes our feelings and our thinking but also a dimension much deeper than both. This dimension of our humanity that lies deeper than thinking and feeling is the inner territory of our spirit. We need to open to the deeper centre of our being.

Much of our problem in the spiritual life comes from our tendency to identify ourselves exclusively with our feelings or our thinking. We believe that these are the qualities which make us human, but all animals have feelings and, at some level, they have some ability to think.

The heart is that deeper hidden inner dimension of human existence where spiritual reality is perceived and where God is known. This is what makes us truly human, created in the image of God.

For many of us this heart dimension has fallen asleep as a result of neglect or abuse. We have so associated life with the physical, mental, and psychological dimensions that we have lost contact with the inner centre of the human realm that the Bible calls the heart. Richard Rohr says, "We have to accept that we share a mass cultural trance, a hypnotic trance. We're all sleep-walkers."[1]

Our hearts need to be reawakened. Jesus called this being born again. When we are born again, our hearts come to life and we are able to see.

How do our hearts come to life? They must be pure. To be pure is to be unmixed. Our hearts are asleep because we are attached to things. In order to allow our hearts to wake up, we need to let go of all attachments and live in God. This is why Jesus said, "You shall love the Lord your God with all your heart, and with all your soul, and with all your mind. This is the greatest and first commandment" (Matthew 22:37, 38).

Meeting God in the heart is the starting place for a Christian spiritual life. Jesus expressed this in the harshest possible terms when he said, "Whoever comes to me and does not hate father and mother, wife and children, brothers and sisters, yes and even life itself, cannot be my disciple. Whoever does not carry the cross and follow me cannot be my disciple (Luke 14:26, 27). To carry the cross of Jesus is to die to all attachments in this world. Jesus said, "No one can serve two masters; for a slave will either hate the one and love the other, or be devoted to the one and despise the other" (Matthew 6:24).

A slave drops absolutely everything the moment the master calls. A slave does not say, "I'll do it when I have time." He drops his own agenda, surrendering his deepest desires to those of the master. However, when the master is the God we meet in our hearts, our surrender brings us true freedom because our Master desires only our greatest well-being.

---

1   Rohr, *Everything Belongs*, p. 28.

Richard Rohr says, "Secular freedom is *having* to do what you *want* to do. Religious freedom is *wanting* to do what you *have* to do."[2] Those whose hearts have been reawakened and reborn know that their greatest delight is found in wanting to do the Master's will. Doing the Master's will makes us pure in heart so that we may see God, and seeing God is the ultimate satisfaction in human life.

You can settle for less. You can settle for seeing your own great achievements or for the comfort and distraction of an entertaining life. But anything less than the full surrender that results in seeing God will always leave you empty, dissatisfied and sad at the centre of your being.

This Beatitude lies at the centre of Jesus' teaching. It challenges us to find our true identity as human beings. It is a call to true freedom when we find our true destiny as embodied forms of God's glory and when we settle for nothing less.

1. What does it mean to "see" in a sense that is deeper than the physical process of sight? What hinders this process of seeing? What helps us to see in this deeper way?

2. What do we understand by the term "heart"? How do we become familiar with this territory of the heart? How might our lives look different if we lived with an awakened heart?

Consider a situation in your life and try to view the situation from that place within yourself which is deeper than thinking or feeling. See how your perspective shifts when you view a situation from this deeper place.

---

2 Ibid., p. 93.

8

Making Peace

Matthew 5:9

Blessed are the peacemakers, for they will be called children of God.

The twentieth century was the most violent, deadly, war torn century in human history. It counted over 100 million civilians dead — 44.4 war-related deaths for every 1,000 people on the planet. The next closest century was the nineteenth in which there were 16.2 deaths per 1,000 people in the world.

All the extraordinary advances in technology, learning, and information gathering of the past century or two appear only to have enabled us to kill more efficiently and to carry on more deadly wars. We have not learned to live more peacefully or with greater mutual respect for the other occupants of this small planet we call home. Our strategies for living together are not working.

Jesus said, "Blessed are the peacemakers, for they will be called children of God."

But how are we to make peace? Will building bigger bombs and stock piling more weapons do the trick? If massive armaments could bring peace, the twentieth century should have been the most peaceful century in history.

The key to peacemaking lies in a little statement Jesus made towards the end of his earthly life. Tensions were beginning to rise. Jesus' disciples, increasingly anxious about the future, were huddled in the upper room with him at the time of Passover. Jesus had just predicted that he was about to be betrayed and that Peter would deny knowing him. Then Jesus reassured his followers that, in spite of the difficulties that lay ahead, they would be all right: "Peace I leave with you; my peace I give to you."

The word to notice here is "my": "my peace I give to you." The first principle of peacemaking is that you cannot make what you do not have. If you do not have peace you cannot make peace.

In November 1943 Etty Hillesum, a young Jewish woman, died in Auschwitz. In the diary she kept during her internment, published in 1983, she wrote:

> Ultimately, we have just one moral duty: to reclaim large areas of peace in ourselves, more and more peace, and to reflect it towards others. And the more peace there is in us, the more peace there will also be in our troubled world.[1]

By our inner state we create the world in which we live. If our hearts are filled with violence, hatred, vengeance, and the need for control, there will be violence and hatred wherever we go.

The question, "Is there peace in your heart?" is not the same as asking whether you want security and protection against

---

1   Etty Hillesum, *Etty: The Letters and Diaries of Etty Hillesum 1941–1943* (Grand Rapids, Michigan: William B. Eerdmans, 2002).

your enemies or even whether you want to make the world a safe place for other people. These are universal human desires. The question means, "Do we know peace within ourselves at the heart of our being where we encounter God? Have we reclaimed 'large areas of peace' within ourselves?"

We can test our own experience: Are our lives driven by anxiety, fear, uncertainty, worry, turmoil, unrest? Are we driven by a need for revenge, the determination to get even at all costs? Or are we sustained by a steady strong base of trust, confidence, rest, and peace?

How can we experience within ourselves that peace we desire to see in the world?

The five Beatitudes we have looked at so far answer this question. But the key is "Blessed are the pure in heart, for they will see God." To be pure in heart is to be unmixed, clean, unattached to anything, but aware of living in God.

Conflict is caused by attachment. A lovely story from the ancient desert tradition of the Christian East makes the point. Two old men lived together for many years without a quarrel. One said, "Let us have one quarrel with each other, as is the way of men."

The other answered, "I do not know how a quarrel happens."

The first explained. "Look, I put a brick between us and I say, 'That's mine.' Then you say, 'No, it's mine.' That is how you begin a quarrel."

So they put a brick between them, and the first said, "That's mine." The other said, "No; it's mine."

Then the first old man replied, "Yes, it is yours. Take it away." And they parted unable to argue with each other.

When we view the world through the eyes of "mine" and "yours," we will do all we can to protect our possessions. The Christian spiritual teacher Cynthia Bourgeault says, "As long as we need life to give us something, we will be violent."[2] Violence stems from our sense of need, demand, expectation, and attachment.

When I am attached to my vision of how my children must turn out, needing them to be a certain way, I will do violence to my children in order achieve my vision for their lives. When I am attached to my goals and purposes, I will feel threatened by anything that gets in the way of achieving these goals. When I expect you to satisfy my longings, I will do violence to you when you fail to meet my expectations.

Attachment is about trying to build a safe world for myself. Attachment is about trying to secure my sense of identity against hostile forces. Attachment demands, *my* rights, *my* privileges, *my* possessions. Attachment is not a path to peace or safety for anyone.

I do violence to myself and to everyone around me when I am determined at all costs to get my way and to make the world conform to my version of reality. Wars are caused by people who are so identified with a particular position that they need to force everyone else to agree with them.

Peacemakers know life is not safe. Jesus said, "Blessed are the peacemakers, for they will be called children of God." Children are vulnerable. If you are going to be a peacemaker, you have to be willing to be vulnerable. There are not enough weapons in all the arsenals of all the military powers of all the world to make the world a perfectly safe place. You get to peace by accepting your vulnerability. You discover peace within by accepting that life often does not turn out as you think it should or as you wish it would. You get to peace when you know that,

---

2   Cynthia Bourgeault, A Public Lecture, 13 November 2003, Victoria, B.C.

whatever happens, no one and nothing can take from you the most important reality in your life.

Followers of Jesus know that there is nothing outside of themselves that can secure their sense of identity or fulfill their deepest longings. Followers of Jesus know that peace only comes as a result of a deep inner transformation.

That transformation involves knowing that you are called children of God. You do not need to create life for yourself. You need only to receive life as a gift. There is nothing to cling to, nothing to protect, nothing to fight for. Safety lies in the security of knowing that when you let go of everything, you discover that you have everything you need or could desire. You are loved. Your life is held in the gracious loving hand of God.

Peace is an inner state of being when we can rest and trust in Christ. No army can threaten and no circumstance can destroy it. This place of inner peace is the only base from which we can move out into the world to be peacemakers.

The world does not need more empires or more technological advances — bigger buildings, faster computers, smarter bombs, or better defence shields. The world needs more peaceful people, who know that there is an alternative reality. The world needs people who can stand aside from the conflict and let go of their agendas, lay down their visions, surrender their wills, and give up their attachments. Jesus calls us to know that we are all children of God who can be bearers of that peace which God alone can give.

1. What are the most common peacemaking strategies that the world uses? How have these worked in bringing about lasting and secure peace? What might be the problem with these strategies?

2. Where might a different version of peacemaking begin? What might a different vision of peacemaking look like? What might we do to contribute to bringing about a new vision of peacemaking?

Identify a spiritual discipline in your life that allows you to "reclaim large areas of peace within yourself." Observe how this peace within you affects your approach to life and changes your relationships.

9

The Blessing
of Suffering

Matthew 5:10–12

Blessed are those who are persecuted for righteousness'
sake, for theirs is the kingdom of heaven. Blessed are
you when people revile you and persecute you and utter
all kinds of evil against you falsely on my account. Re-
joice and be glad, for your reward is great in heaven, for
in the same way they persecuted the prophets who were
before you.

You have to feel a certain sympathy for the public relations
firm that was responsible for handling Jesus' image. The spin-
doctors must have wrung their hands as they listened to Jesus'
teaching and watched him perform under the close scrutiny of
the public eye.

What do you do with someone who, in his most extended
public teaching, says outrageous things like, "Blessed are the
poor in spirit... Blessed are those who mourn... Blessed are
those who hunger and thirst...?" You can imagine Jesus' speech
writers saying, "Wait a minute. He's departing from the text
again. He's improvising. This is not what we told him to say."

Then, as if this is not bad enough, Jesus concludes his crazy list of keys to happiness by adding, "Blessed are those who are persecuted." And just to make sure you don't miss the point, for the first time in all eight Beatitudes, Jesus chooses to expand this one, saying,

> Blessed are you when people revile you and persecute you and utter all kinds of evil against you falsely on my account. Rejoice and be glad, for your reward is great in heaven, for in the same way they persecuted the prophets who were before you.

Back to the spin doctors. How do they sell this bleak, depressing message to the average individual who is just looking for a little bit of encouragement and affirmation? And how do we respond?

One option would be to say that this text as written has no real application in our lives. Most of us are not going to be reviled, persecuted, and have all kinds of evil spoken against us falsely just because of our faith in Jesus, although these things may happen to us for reasons other than our faith. There are places in the world today where persecution is a reality for Christians. But few people in the Western world can legitimately lay claim to having faced the kind of persecution that Jesus is speaking about here.

Jesus knew that the most immediate form of suffering his disciples would experience was persecution for their faith. But Jesus has chosen persecution as a symbol for suffering in general. It is always going to hurt to admit that you are poor in spirit. It is going to be painful to mourn for the brokenness of the world and the brokenness of our own lives. To hunger and thirst for the presence of God, to practice mercy, to be so detached from the things of this world that you can be pure in heart, to be peacemakers — these are all going to involve personal pain and suffering.

This may not be a popular message. It may not fill churches or sell lots of books. But Jesus was more committed to truth than to making people feel good or encouraging them to live a life of illusion and lies. He knew that, when we live by his kingdom principles instead of by the ways of the world, we will experience discomfort.

In this Beatitude Jesus is not talking about the suffering caused by our foolish choices or by our arrogance, dishonesty, or inability to let go and accept the realities of life. Here Jesus is talking about suffering for righteousness' sake. This is suffering that comes about as a result of living by the presence of God. It is suffering undergone on account of Jesus and our commitment to living in faithful obedience to his teaching.

This unique kind of suffering brings blessing, yet it certainly does not feel like blessing at the time. When people are uttering "all kinds of evil against you falsely on my account," it does not feel like a blessing or a reward.

What is the reward that comes from living by the Beatitudes?

There are times when all our spiritual practice does not seem to make our lives any better or any more rewarding than an ordinary life lived with no reference to God at all. However, we need to know that, if we are looking for the rewards of the spiritual life in the realm of feelings, we are looking in the wrong place. This is why it is so easy to fall away from spiritual practice. If we are hoping to get good feelings from our spiritual practice, we will give up when those good feelings vanish, as they inevitably will. Our relationship with God is not about feelings.

Thomas Merton was a man who, by all reports, lived in deep and profound communion with God. Yet speaking about the place of feelings in a relationship with God, Merton wrote:

We must remember that our experience of union with God, our feeling of His presence, is altogether accidental and secondary. It is only a side effect of His actual presence in our souls, and gives no sure indication of that presence in any case. For God Himself is above all apprehension and ideas and sensations, however spiritual, that can ever be experienced by the spirit of man in this life.[1]

The Bible is consistent in bearing witness to the fact that God does not always come to us as a warm comforting glow. We must look elsewhere for our apprehension of God, as Merton says, "above all apprehension and ideas and sensations, however spiritual."

Jesus says those "who are persecuted for righteousness' sake are blessed for theirs is the kingdom of heaven." He says "your reward is great in heaven." Jesus used the terms "heaven" and "kingdom of heaven" to refer to a whole new dimension of life, "above all apprehension and ideas and sensations." To follow Jesus is to live in the "above" state all the way to heaven.

In Luke 17:21, Jesus says, "the kingdom of God is inside you." This may not be exactly how your Bible translates the verse, but it is a good translation. The kingdom in which we are rewarded for our suffering is a deep inner realm of being. It is that dimension of human existence which is deeper than feelings, deeper than thoughts, deeper than all the external trappings of life that so often preoccupy us.

If we are going to live the Beatitudes, we must become familiar with this inner, spiritual centre at the heart of our lives.

---

1 Thomas Merton, *No Man Is An Island* (London: Harcourt Brace & Company, 1955), p. 225.

We must get to know the hidden secret inner realm of the human spirit, which is the place where we encounter God. You cannot live the Beatitudes if your life is governed by feelings or by rational thinking, or by any external circumstances.

In the ordinary realm of human affairs, the teachings of Jesus are not reasonable, practical, or even sensible. They conflict over and over with our feelings, but we do not live by our feelings or by the standards and norms of the world. We live by the Spirit of God, who lives in the innermost centre of our lives.

1. How have you experienced the suffering that is an inevitable outcome of living by the spiritual principles of the Beatitudes? What have been the long term effects of this suffering in your life and in your relationships?

2. What will our lives look like if we give primary consideration to the "hidden secret inner realm of the human spirit" where God is known?

When you experience suffering, instead of recoiling as though something strange were happening, see your suffering as a gift. Observe how your suffering is calling you to a deeper place, beneath feelings, thinking, or any sensation. Respond to your suffering by resting in this deeper place of trust and gratitude.

The Lord's Prayer

1

Resting On God's Chest

Matthew 6:9 (i)

Our Father...

Matthew 6:9–13 is probably the most universally familiar passage in the entire Bible. Even in nominally Christian circles, if you mention the Lord's Prayer, most people have some awareness of what you are talking about. But familiarity with the words does not guarantee that any of us really understands the content of this complex passage of Scripture.

The difficulty of dealing with this passage is increased by the challenges of translation. The Hebrew Scriptures, which we know as the Old Testament, were written, for the most part, in Hebrew. The Christian New Testament was written in Greek. However, to make our understanding of the Lord's Prayer even more difficult, the words of this prayer were originally spoken by Jesus in Aramaic. So when we read the Lord's Prayer, we are reading an English translation of a written Greek translation of an orally transmitted Aramaic original.

The challenges this poses can be seen immediately when we consider the first word in the Lord's Prayer: "Our." Beginning with mention of ourselves may cause us to think that we are the starting point of Christian faith. In fact, the prayer begins with God. The Greek version from which we get our English translations does not say, "Our Father;" it says *Pater hemon*," that is, "Father of us." The starting point is God, not me.

Consider the connection with the first four words in most English translations of the Book of Genesis: "In the beginning God." Appearances to the contrary, we human beings are not the centre of the universe. Healthy spirituality begins with finding the real centre. The Wisdom for which we long will only be uncovered if we start there.

God is the centre of all existence. God is the reason for Creation. Creation is an expression of the Being of the God who created all that is.

The God known to us in Jesus Christ is not only the source and origin of all Creation, but also continues to be deeply involved in and connected to the Creation. If one of my children came to me and said, "Good morning, Oh Source of my life," I might feel this to be an inadequate description of our relationship. I want to be more to my children than simply the source to which they trace their origin.

I recently heard the story of an infant born prematurely and suffering from a variety of life-threatening complications. As a result of her difficult birth, this tiny newborn spent the first few months of life in an incubator. If you have ever seen an infant in an incubator in the intensive care nursery of a hospital, you know it is not a cosy, comforting sight. This little girl lay day after day on the bare flat mat at the bottom of her plexiglass home, with tubes running into her body. No one could pick her up. Her parents could only occasionally stroke her fragile little body by reaching into the incubator with long plastic gloves attached to its sides.

During these difficult weeks, her parents developed a habit of prayer in which they imagined their tiny daughter resting on God's chest. Rather than lying on the flat, impersonal bottom of an incubator, they pictured her peacefully sleeping on the soft comforting chest of her heavenly Father. For weeks and weeks every day, her parents routinely held their daughter in this vision of God's care.

Eventually, the baby began to grow stronger until finally she was able to come home with her family. Over the following months and then years, she grew into a healthy little girl. Eventually the family stopped talking about their daughter's difficult first months and their unique practice of praying for their sick baby.

One summer evening when she was five, the little girl was sitting outside on the deck with her mother. As a soft summer breeze blew up, she said to her mother, "Mummy, do you smell that sweet smell?" Her mother replied, "Yes, it's honeysuckle." "No," the little five year old replied, "it's the smell of resting on God's chest."

That is the relationship Jesus invites us into in the Lord's Prayer. Jesus invites us into a relationship in which we come to the place where we are able to smell the fragrance of "resting on God's chest." As the Archbishop of Canterbury, Rowan Williams has written, "The joy which is Jesus' can only be the awareness of being held absolutely in the gaze of the Father, receiving moment by moment the completeness of his love."[1]

When we pray "Father of us," we affirm this relationship of deep intimacy, tenderness, and trust. Our hearts long to know this deep personal relationship of love. All of our striving is

---

1   Rowan Williams, *Christ On Trial: How The Gospel Unsettles Our Judgment* (Grand Rapids Michigan: Zondervan, 2000), p. 90.

simply our attempt to know ourselves as "held absolutely in the gaze of the Father." Our fears, our insecurities, and our anxieties exist only because we forget to dwell in this place of "resting on God's chest."

To pray "Father of us" is to enter this deep rest. It is to express faith and trust that this rest is the goal and purpose of human existence. There is nowhere else we want to be, nothing else we want to do. All true prayer, all healthy life, flows from "resting on God's chest." Jesus' prayer starts in this place of rest. So our lives need to start from this centre of security and confidence that is God.

We live in a frightening world. A sniper in Washington, D.C., defiantly threatens, "Your children are not safe anywhere at any time." And he is right. Where can we hide from the bullets of a sniper? A young father walks off the soccer field at half time with chest pains. His children watch as an ambulance rushes him to emergency suffering from a heart attack.

The only safety we can ever know is the safety we experience within. The inner safety that comes from praying "Father of us" tells us that no matter what may happen, there is a centre within every human being deeper and more peaceful than any circumstance life may bring. The relationship we have with God is stronger, more sure, and more secure than all the things in life that frighten us. No threat can ever take from us that core which is our most true self, revealed to us in Jesus.

<hr />

1. What is the impact on our personal lives, other people, and the world around us of viewing human beings as "the starting point of Christian faith"? What might begin to cause this perspective to shift?

2. What practices might help us stay connected to the deep inner centre at the heart of our being, which is the source of all true strength, security, and human identity?

At random throughout your day, stop for a moment; take a deep breath. Rest; be still. Relax your hands and your shoulders. Feel your feet on the ground. Sense within yourself, the deep well-spring of life, which is your true being.

2

Praying in Two Dimensions

Matthew 6:9 (ii)

Our Father in heaven...

My father died twenty years ago. He was seventy-three when he died; I was twenty-nine and unable to admit that he was really my father. I don't mean I doubted my biological parentage. But at twenty-nine, I was still determined to convince the world I was not really my father's son.

My father was an Anglican priest. One of my strongest memories from childhood is of nice people patting me on the head saying, "When you grow up, you are going to be just like your Daddy." They meant well, but I spent a lot of years trying to prove them wrong.

Well, in the end they were proved right. The similarities between the man I have become and the man my father was are unnerving. You may have heard the expression, "The apple does not fall very far from the tree." My children — any children — may not want to hear it, but children are like their parents.

So, when Jesus instructs us to pray "Our Father," he is telling us that there is something in our nature that is like God.

The First Letter of John says, "See what love the Father has given us, that we should be called children of God; and that is what we are" (I John 3:1). Since we are children of God, there is that within us which bears the indelible stamp of God. Our true nature is to be like the God in whose image we were made.

The great fourth century Greek theologian Gregory of Nazianzus describes the extraordinary dignity and richness of the human part of Creation:

> The Word of God took a lump of newly created earth, formed it with his immortal hands into our shape, and imparted life to it: for the spirit that he breathed into it is a flash of the invisible godhead. Thus from clay and breath was created humanity, the image of the Immortal.[1]

The centre of our nature is that "flash of the invisible." At the core of our being is "the image of the Immortal."

We can fight against our nature all we want, but in the end we cannot change our inheritance. I am my father's son. I am a child of God. When I pray "Our Father," I claim my true identity, describing who I really am and to whom my life belongs. It makes sense to live in harmony with my true identity, rather than fight against it.

The problems we experience in life and in our world all stem from the fact that we lose touch with our true identity. Jesus placed at the beginning of his prayer a reminder of our true nature. We are identified with God.

---

1   Quoted in Olivier Clement, *The Roots of Christian Mysticism* (New York: New City Press, 1993), p. 79.

But it is important not to stop here. The Greek text of the prayer says, *"Pater hemon"* ("God of us"). It then adds, *"en tois ouranois"* ("in the heavens"). There is similarity between us and God. But there are also differences. God is "in the heavens."

This expression needs careful consideration. Many people think of heaven as some distant place, far removed from the physical realm, where God dwells outside time. They tend to think of it as "apple pie in the sky in the sweet by and by," a realm, hopefully in the far distant future, where we will receive our reward for having put up with the drudgery of life.

Although there is a future dimension to the biblical understanding of heaven, this is not an adequate picture of all the Bible means when it speaks about heaven.

To get a fuller grasp of the term "heaven," we need to go back to Matthew 4:17 where Jesus said, "Repent, for the kingdom of heaven is at hand" (English Standard Version). The same Greek word "at hand" appears again at the end of Matthew. Jesus has been praying in the Garden of Gethsemani while his disciples slept: "Then Jesus came to the disciples and said to them, "Sleep and take your rest later on. See, the hour is at hand, and the Son of Man is betrayed" (Matthew 26:45, *ESV*). In both these cases the expression "is at hand" means "here and now."

When we pray, "Our Father in heaven" we are affirming not only our ultimate destiny after physical life, but also God's living presence here and now. God is at hand.

God dwells within us and yet embraces all that is. God is the life force who flows through all life and yet transcends all life forms. God is both the life dancing in all that is and the music that surrounds the dance of life. The God of Christian faith is both within and beyond all forms of life. We express this awareness in the word "heaven."

When we use the word "heaven," we are talking about a

dimension of reality that is both beyond time and yet is also present at all times and in all places. To see this dimension of existence in which God is always present requires eyes of faith and a trusting heart. The fact that we may not always perceive it does not mean it is not there or is not real. It simply means that the ordinary course of life has taught us not to see it.

But we can learn. When I was a child, I could not see my father as the man he was. I saw him only through the eyes of my rebellion, through the pitiful little filter of my arrogance. Now that some of my rebellious nature has been gentled a little, I am able to see a different dimension in the man who was responsible for the beginning of my physical life.

When we celebrate All Saints Day and All Souls Day, remembering people who have died, we affirm their continued existence even though we no longer see them physically. They exist more fully now in that invisible realm which is always present. We remind ourselves that the separation between what is and what will be is much thinner than we think. The distance between us now and the saints who have died is small because the whole of life and death is caught up in God.

When we pray "Our Father in heaven," we acknowledge that God is the God of everything and that everything we see, feel, hear and touch is just another indicator of the presence of the living God. By praying the Lord's Prayer we open ourselves to that other dimension, affirming that the transcendent realm of Being is found in us.

Deluded by the surface of life, we think what we see today is all there is because it is all we see. The Lord's Prayer invites us to see into a deeper reality with the inner eye of the heart. It asks that we let go of the rational, linear thinking that characterizes our Western culture and move to a deeper place, where God is seen to fill all reality.

1. How do we see "the indelible stamp of God" in our lives and in the lives of others? What is the effect upon our feelings, for ourselves and for others, of seeing this image of God in the human dimension of Creation?

2. How can we open our eyes to the "hidden inner dimension of life"? How can we encourage one another to have open eyes? What might a community look like that is made up of people who live with their eyes open to this depth dimension of life?

Pay attention to your life. Notice the details. Become conscious of the more subtle dimension of Being that exists at the centre of all Creation. Share with another person those moments when you became aware of being conscious of a deeper dimension to life.

3

Part of the Family

Our Father in heaven…

At the beginning of the Lord's Prayer Jesus instructs us to pray *pater hemon*, "Father of us." Each word is important. We start with God but we declare that this God is "of us."

The "us" is extremely significant. The speaker is Jesus, who was introduced in Matthew's gospel by John the Baptist:

> One who is more powerful than I is coming after me whose sandals I am not worthy to carry. He will baptize you with the Holy Spirit and with fire. His winnowing fork is in his hand, and he will clear his threshing floor and will gather his wheat into the granary, but the chaff he will burn with unquenchable fire (Matthew 3:11–12).

John's portrait of Jesus presents a person of such extraordinary power and exalted status that John is not even worthy to perform the menial tasks of a slave for him.

The first thing we notice about most powerful people is that they keep their distance. When the Queen visited my hometown, few people had the opportunity to walk up and shake her hand. The Queen is protected, cut off from mere mortals like us. Yet this great person Jesus, when he instructs his followers to pray *pater hemon*, "Father of us," is saying that we share the same Father and belong with him in the same family.

Mark's gospel presents an intriguing incident in Jesus' life. Jesus is in a house surrounded by a great crowd when someone announces that Jesus' mother and brothers are outside the door. Jesus "replied, 'Who are my mother and my brothers?'"And looking about at those who sat around him, he said, "Here are my mother and my brothers! Whoever does the will of God is my brother and sister and mother'" (Mark 3:33–35). When we pray "Father of us," we affirm that we belong to the family of Jesus Christ.

We need to notice that we cannot pray the Lord's Prayer alone. We do not pray "My Father," but "Our Father." The community of all those who are brothers and sisters of Jesus is always included in our prayer.

What does it mean for us to be family members with Jesus? And, even more significantly, what does it mean for us to be family members with one another?

The primate of the Anglican Church of Australia, Archbishop Peter Carnley, made this comment following a terrorist bombing in Bali in which many Australian tourists were included among the victims: "The importance of our common life together in the church, transcending as it does natural divisions of class, gender, or ethnic difference, is that it is a concrete and visible sign of the kingdom of human unity, justice, and peace for men and women of all races and nations."

Anyone can pray "Our Father," and anyone who does belongs to "us." We may not like all the people who pray "Our Father," and we may not agree on every detail of doctrine or ethics, but we are all connected. Like Archbishop Carnley, I believe this may be the most important thing the church can say today.

Increasingly our world is fracturing, breaking apart on the shoals of special interest. Everywhere we look we see the human community dividing along ideological, ethnic, geographical, economic and, most tragically of all, even religious lines. The church needs to be a sign that it is possible to be together in community with people with whom we might not naturally get along. It is possible to overlook differences and to disagree on even quite important issues, yet still remain together in Christ because we join Jesus in praying "Our Father." In Jesus we have a unity that transcends differences. We have a connection that is deeper even than disagreement.

When we pray "Our Father," we say we are family. It is a profound tragedy when families break apart. Everything in Jesus' Sermon on the Mount, of which the Lord's Prayer is a part, aims at encouraging us to acknowledge that we belong together as we continue in the journey of faith.

As the world more and more breaks apart, we need to show that it is possible to reverse the trend. It is possible to rise above the dissension and disharmony that characterize so much of public discourse in our day. The violence of division does not need to infect those who pray "Our Father."

1. How do we make real in our lives the family relationships to which we commit ourselves when we pray "Our Father?" What barriers might there be in our lives and our communities to fully realizing this family relationship?

2. What will it require for the church to be a sign to the world that it is possible for people in communities to continue in communion with one another regardless of differences and even disagreements?

Find a person in the church with whom you experience a significant disagreement. Concentrate on finding ways that you can identify commonality with this person. Focus on the common ground you share, looking together beyond your differences.

4

Seeing Clearly

Matthew 6:9 (iv)

Hallowed be your name.

After "Our Father in heaven" we pray "hallowed be your name." This is where things get demanding. The only place where this part of the prayer can be answered is in our own lives. It is not God who is going to hallow God's name. This is our job.

What does it mean for us to "hallow" God's name? What does it mean for us to be the answer to this part of Jesus' prayer?

In Jesus' culture the name stood for the whole person: your name is you and your name evokes your presence. So in this prayer we are asking that God's presence be hallowed. To "hallow" is to "make holy or to make pure." But God is already holy and pure beyond anything we can contribute.

But remember that this is a prayer to which *we* are the answer. We are really praying that God's presence may be hallowed in the lives of those who pray the prayer. In other words, God's name is hallowed when we are purified; and we are purified when we are willing to carve out space for God to dwell in our lives.

Our lives are a confusing jumble filled with clutter, distractions, divided loyalties, and complicated motivations. When we pray the Lord's Prayer, we are praying that this jumble in our lives may be addressed.

According to Matthew's account, just before his death Jesus went into the temple in Jerusalem and cleaned out the money changers:

> Jesus entered the temple and drove out all who were selling and buying in the temple, and he overturned the tables of the money changers and the seats of those who sold doves. He said to them, "It is written, 'My house shall be called a house of prayer'; but you are making it a den of robbers" (Matthew 21:12, 13).

Our inner lives have become dens of robbers. We have allowed things into our lives which rob us of our true nature. We have allowed things to rob us of "love, joy, peace, patience, kindness, generosity, faithfulness, gentleness, and self-control" (Galatians 5:22, 23). These are our true heritage as children created in the image of God.

The Lord's Prayer challenges us to drive the money-changers and the sellers of doves out of the temple of our lives. This we can do by looking into our hearts and asking a fundamental spiritual question: What are those things which make it difficult for us to clear a space in which we can see the living, pure, and holy presence of God? We'll likely find that in our cluttered lives we have hallowed achievement, busyness, glamour, and personal comfort. We have failed to hallow God.

The Lord's Prayer starts with a challenge to let go of those needs, wants, desires, demands, and expectations that fill the temple of our spirits and make it impossible for us to see God. To say "hallowed be your name" is to commit ourselves to house cleaning and to ask that the grit be removed from our eyes so that we may see with unclouded vision.

The Christian spiritual journey is not going out to find God.

The Psalmist inquires of God, "Where can I go from your spirit? Or where can I flee from your presence?" then answers his own question:

> If I ascend to heaven, you are there! If I make my bed in Sheol, you are there! If I take the wings of the morning and settle at the farthest limits of the sea, even there your hand shall lead me, and your right hand shall hold me fast (Psalm 139:7–10).

There is nowhere God is not. Even if you are not aware of God's presence, this does not mean God is absent. Where there is life there is God. When we pray "Our Father in heaven," we affirm that God's presence permeates all of reality.

The only issue is whether or not we are willing to make space to see what truly is. Are we willing to let go and live in God alone? Are we willing to stop pursuing the illusions that have driven our lives and recognize that only in God will we find our true nature and the true meaning of our lives? When we clean out the clutter, that which is more truly our nature will naturally be revealed at the innermost centre of our being.

When we pray "Our Father" we say, "I am a child of God. My nature therefore is to live in relation to my true Father." It is a sad thing when a child makes herself an orphan. Nothing we cling to is worth making ourselves an orphan for. The saddest things in life come from loneliness and a sense that as people we don't really matter. When we know our true identity as children of God, we are set free from these afflictions. Our only need is to open, to receive the awareness of God's living presence in our lives.

The Lord's Prayer invites us to leave our orphaned condition and, hallowing God's name, to come back to the awareness of our true nature as those who are created by and filled with the living presence of God.

1. What are some of the "wrong things" we may have "hallowed" in our lives? What is the impact of this "hallowing"?

2. What is it going to require for us to "carve out space for God to dwell" in our lives? What things and activities might we need to let go of, in order for there to be more space for God? Are we willing to make this sacrifice?

Be conscious of allowing space in your life. Don't rush instantly to burst into every conversation of which you are a part. Be aware of the stillness and the silence that your words will interrupt. Allow for space in your relationships with other people. Expand this spacious place within yourself to embrace more of life.

5

The Kingdom That Is and Isn't

Matthew 6:10 (i)

Your kingdom come...

We have seen that, when we pray "hallowed be your name," our lives are the only possible answer to our prayer. When we pray "your kingdom come," we are acknowledging that we are then called to go out and fulfill the prayer. We are committing ourselves to taking personal responsibility for our lives.

It may not have been immediately obvious to us that this is the meaning of "your kingdom come" because the prayer is confusing. The word "kingdom" appears 162 times in the New Testament. When the New Testament speaks of the kingdom of God, it is referring to God's rule. The kingdom of God is where God is in charge.

But the New Testament seems to be confused about God's reign in human affairs. Sometimes it seems to suggest that God's kingdom is not entirely present here in this world and we should wait for it. In our own experience we certainly see many parts of life that do not seem to conform fully to God's will.

However, at the same time the New Testament speaks of God's kingdom as if, in Jesus, it has already been established and is a present reality in all of life. So, if the kingdom of God has already come, why does Jesus tell us that we should pray that God's kingdom *might* come?

We need to acknowledge that God's reign over this world has not yet been perfectly fulfilled. Bad things happen. Life is messy. We know that there are broken things in life. We know that there are times when we do things we cannot explain, times when our behaviour does not make good sense. There are parts of our lives which are not fully submitted to God. When we pray "your kingdom come," we express our awareness of all this and our longing that we may no longer hurt one another. We cry out to God with longing that the day may come when we conform more fully to the life-giving will of our Creator.

But we also recognize that at a deeper place, it *is* true to say that, in spite of the brokenness all around us, God's reign has come in Christ. In fact, some scholars suggest that the original Aramaic in which Jesus spoke this prayer means, "Your kingdom *is* come." In Matthew 12:28, Jesus says, "The kingdom of God has come to you." In Luke 17:21, Jesus says, "In fact, the kingdom of God is among you." That for which we long has in fact been realized. God does reign.

So the prayer says two things at once: "God's kingdom is coming" and "God's kingdom has come." God's rule, though not fully realized in the world, is yet present in all of life. We know this from experience. There are aspects of our lives that are confused, chaotic, dark, and beyond our limited understanding, and at the same time there is a dimension of our lives that is pure and true and whole.

Problems arise when we start to believe only one or other of these positions. Looking at the state of the worlds we could be forgiven for thinking that there really is only mess. We are often overwhelmingly aware of the absence of God's kingdom and of the brokenness. So we are apt to believe that brokenness, pain, and suffering are the only reality.

If brokenness is the only reality, then it probably won't be long before I will start to believe that I am responsible for fixing it all. In the absence of God's kingdom and in the face of the irrefutable tragedy of much of life, I will feel pressure to clean up the mess, establish my own kingdom here on earth, and make things safe and secure. I will start to believe that my vision of the world is the one that is so obviously missing and must prevail.

But when I pray "your kingdom come," I accept that the kingdom for which I pray is God's kingdom. And God's kingdom is not entirely here now. There is always going to be some mess in this life. My vision of life is only partial. When I accept that what is missing and must prevail is God's kingdom, I surrender my need for tidiness. I give up trying to build my own little kingdom of security and predictability.

I am not sure that I am entirely ready to give up my kingdom just yet. Part of me still thinks, if only I work a little harder, I will be able to fix things. I will be able to get rid of all the mess in my life and perhaps even in the whole world.

But I am not responsible for fixing my world. I can't do it anyway. If I were responsible for fixing my life, then pretty soon I would start lying to myself, denying those broken parts of my being, and turning a blind eye to the mess in my life. All of a sudden I would no longer be able to face my own brokenness. This is a dangerous place to be. But when we pray "your kingdom come," we acknowledge our need for continuing transformation and change in our own lives.

In fact, there is only one kingdom and one King. If I recognize that I am not the king of any domain, I can accept the mess in my life and in the world because God's kingdom has come and is still coming. God is in charge. God's purposes are being worked out.

When we pray "your kingdom come," we are asking God to open our eyes to reality. We are asking God to remind us of the truth of God's rule over all of life. We are acknowledging that we are not in control and that we do not actually need to be in control because God's kingdom is here.

It is a big, big prayer. By praying it we are choosing to surrender control of our being to the Maker of our being. We are acknowledging our helplessness to reconstruct our lives out of the chaos we have all created. We are laying down our determination to be in control. We are accepting that life can at times be difficult, confusing, even bleak. And still we choose to trust in the King who rules ultimately in the kingdom of God.

<hr />

1. How do we relate to the messiness of life? What is our response when we see brokenness around us, in our own lives, in the lives of those with whom we have contact, and in the wider world? What happens when we take it upon ourselves to attempt to fix the brokenness of life?

2. In the midst of the chaos, confusion, and conflict that so often characterizes much of life, how can we maintain our awareness that "the kingdom of God has come"? How does this awareness affect our behaviour in response to the reality of brokenness?

Watch for mess in your life. Just observe it; don't judge it. Don't rush to try to tidy everything up in your life. See what happens to the mess when you just watch it and let it be for a while. When you see mess, remember you are more than the messes in your life.

6

Two Wills or One?

Matthew 6:10 (ii)

Your will be done, on earth as it is in heaven.

In Matthew 6:10, having instructed us to pray "your kingdom come," Jesus goes on in the second half of the verse to defines God's kingdom, telling us to pray, "your will be done, on earth as it is in heaven." God's kingdom is the place where God's "will" is done.

When we pray "your will be done," we imply the possibility that there might be a will other than God's. The New Testament is clear that, even for Jesus, all human beings have two wills, not just one. In the Garden of Gethsemani, Jesus prayed, "Father, if you are willing, remove this cup from me; yet, not my will, but yours, be done" (Luke 22:42). In John's gospel, Jesus is reported to have said, "I have come down from heaven, not to do my own will, but the will of him who sent me" (John 6:38).

This is the fundamental human dilemma. We are divided people, often facing in two different directions at the same time. Paul describes our situation perfectly in Romans where he says, "I do not understand my own actions. For I do not do what I want, but I do the very thing I hate" (Romans 7:15). It is as if we are two people, one within who wants to live in God's freedom and another who remains bound to other choices.

Most of us know what it feels like to be torn in two. We know what it feels like to desperately long for that chocolate chip cookie and at the same time desperately not want to eat it. We know what it feels like to stand in the store craving that shiny new computer and knowing we should not spend the money right now. We know what it feels like to hear ourselves responding bitterly to someone we love and wishing we could respond differently.

To pray "your will be done" is to express our desire that the person within us who desires to live in conformity with God may win, that we may be conformed to God's will, not our own. Jesus calls us to lay down the little will of our self-interest and to take up the single will of God. Jesus prayed in Gethesemani, "Father, if you are willing, remove this cup from me. Nevertheless, not my will, but yours, be done" (Luke 22:42).

The problem with our small self-will is its belief that God shares our obsession with external circumstances. But God does not appear to be terribly concerned with making sure that the circumstances of our lives work out smoothly and easily. God seems to be more concerned that the reality of heaven, of the invisible realm, should be manifest in the visible realm of earthly affairs. That is why we pray, "your will be done on earth as in heaven."

When we pray the Lord's Prayer, we are committing ourselves to living on this visible earth by the standards, priorities, measurements, and dictates of the invisible realm of God. We are affirming one will over two — the one that agrees with *The Little Prince*, who says, "The thing that is important is the thing that is not seen...."[1]

---

1   Antoine de Saint Exupery, *The Little Prince* (New York: Harcourt, Brace & World, 1971), p. 103.

When I am torn in two, it is because I have fallen prey to the illusion that the visible is the most important. I have believed the illusion that getting a promotion at work is going to satisfy the longing of my heart. I have bought the lie that being married, or not being married, or being married to someone else, or having more money, or living somewhere else, or having different children, or not having children at all, will make me happy.

But God's concern is with the directions of our whole lives. The prophet Micah asks, "What does the Lord require of you?" The answer is not that God requires you to find the right job, the right partner in life, or the right medium to express your talents, but "to do justice, and to love kindness, and to walk humbly with your God" (Micah 6:8).

God is concerned that, if I become a teacher, I be the kind of person who reveals life to those I teach. God desires that, whatever business I might spend my days engaged in, I do it with justice, kindness, and humility. God's will is that, regardless of external circumstances, I might demonstrate in everything I do that the invisible reality of God is the centre of my being and of all existence. The details of my external circumstances are just not that important.

One of the Bible's fundamental messages is that, if we hope to find satisfaction in life by changing our external circumstances, we will always be disappointed.

Jesus said to his disciples, "I have food to eat that you do not know about" (John 4:32). They were fixated on nourishing their bodies, focused on the outer world of external circumstance, and hoping Jesus would fix it by bringing a new political order and solving the problems of war, strife, disharmony, poverty, and unrest. But Jesus did not come to solve problems; he came to create new people. Jesus came to enable human beings to live transformed lives, and transformation only happens from the inside out.

It is not that Jesus did not care about human suffering. He was deeply compassionate and caring. But he knew that true change always starts within when we choose to align our hearts with the invisible realm of God's kingdom; that is, when we choose "your will be done."

When we pray "your will be done," we are laying down our will and surrendering that small harping voice of self-interest which always wants to do it my way, to live by my standards, to do my own thing, to decide for myself how my life should be run regardless of its impact on anyone or anything around me.

Perhaps it feels scary to give up our determination to have our own way. Perhaps we are not sure we want to surrender our will. Perhaps we are still convinced that we actually know better than God how our lives should be run and what is best for us. Perhaps we still really want to build our own little kingdom.

Well, we do not need to be afraid. Jesus said that God only wants one thing for all people: "I came that they may have life, and have it abundantly" (John 10:10). When we trade our will for God's will, we are trading a pitiful little sack of sand for a treasure chest of gold. God's one will is the treasure chest of gold. Living in tune with God's will is the only source of abundant life. All the things I use my will to achieve will eventually vanish in the mist. Only those qualities that grow in my innermost being as a result of conforming to God's will last for eternity.

When I surrender my own will, the inner invisible reality of God's Spirit is released in my life and I am born again from above. Then God's will is done on earth as in heaven.

1. Think of, or describe, an experience when you felt "torn in two." What does this experience feel like? What happens when you have this experience?

2. What happens when we are all trying to build our own little kingdoms? What does it feel like to imagine giving up building our own little kingdoms? How might our lives look different if we gave up struggling to build our own little kingdom?

Pay attention to those moments when you become conscious that a conflict of two wills is present. Notice which will is coming from the smaller self-will of the ego and which will seems to come from a larger more open place. Try to let go of that smaller will and embrace the larger will.

7

Real Bread

〈꞊ᴥ꞊〉

Matthew 6:11 (i)

Give us today our daily bread.

〈꞊ᴥ꞊〉

If you were asked to pick the most difficult request in the Lord's Prayer, you probably would not suggest Matthew 6:11 — "Give us today our daily bread." Most of us probably assume that in this short petition we are simply asking God to provide us with the things we need to sustain life.

However, most of us do not worry much about having enough to eat each day. We probably worry more about not eating too much. In our context, if we are only praying that our stomachs may be full, this prayer is irrelevant.

But for many people this prayer could be deeply offensive. In the 1998 UNICEF report entitled "Focus On Nutrition," Kofi Annan, the UN Secretary-General, wrote that "malnutrition contributes to more than half of the nearly 12 million under-five deaths in developing countries each year."[1] If roughly

---

1   Kofi A. Annan, "The State of the World's Children 1998, Focus on Nutrition" (Unicef Bulletin: http://www.unicef.org/sowc98/).

six million children under the age of five die every year as a result of hunger, that means 16,438 children under the age of five die every day. In a world where this is the reality, how dare those of us who go to bed every night with our stomachs full pray that God may feed us.

In this petition Jesus was considering something much more significant than simply satisfying our physical needs. In order to see what the issue is, we need to look at a translation problem: the word that has traditionally been translated as "daily." The Greek word is *epiousion*. The translation "daily" is redundant; if we pray "give us today," why do we need to add "daily?" In a prayer which is so sparse in its use of words, it seems unlikely Jesus would have wasted his breath and our prayer time qualifying bread that we ask for "this day" by reminding God that it should be given "daily."

Unfortunately, it is difficult to be sure about any translation for *epiousion*. The word appears only twice in the New Testament, here and again in Luke 11:3 in exactly the same context, Luke's version of the Lord's Prayer. Scholars used to think that it was a made-up word, created by the gospel writers to translate Jesus' original Aramaic into Greek. This theory, however, has been disproved since the word *epiousion* has been discovered in at least one ancient Greek manuscript other than the New Testament.

So the question is, what kind of bread is *epiousion* bread? The best way to answer this question is to break the word into its component parts. *Epi* means "upon" and *ousion* means "substance, being, or essence." So it appears that we are asking God for the bread upon which our essence, our substance, or our being depends. This is to say, we are asking God for bread which feeds not our physical bodies, but our inner spiritual being. We are asking for what the Orthodox scholar Alexander

Schmemann has called "substantive" bread.[2]

Paul says that "If there is a physical body, there is also a spiritual body" (I Corinthians 15:44b) Just as our physical body needs food, so does our spiritual body. In praying "give us this day our *substantive* bread," we are not asking for bread for our physical bodies but for our spiritual bodies — bread that sustains and nurtures our inner being, our essence, our true innermost Self.

When Jesus was tempted in the wilderness at the beginning of Matthew's gospel, we are told that, after fasting forty days and forty nights, "he was famished" (Matthew 4:2). Surely we are to understand here that Jesus' physical body was hungry. Therefore Satan's first temptation makes sense: "The tempter came and said to him, 'If you are the Son of God, command these stones to become loaves of bread' " (Matthew 4:3). There must have been a profound temptation for Jesus to use the powers God had given him to satisfy the needs of his body.

One of the fundamental temptations that faces all human beings is feeling that we need to make our own food. We do not believe God will really feed us. So we go looking for ways to nurture ourselves. We confuse the physical realm with the spiritual, assuming that if we accomplish things in the physical realm, this will satisfy the spiritual dimension of our being. But it does not. We live in a culture that is fed physically with an abundance of "food" but is dying of spiritual malnutrition.

Paul goes on to remind us that "flesh and blood cannot inherit the kingdom of God, nor does the perishable inherit the imperishable" (I Corinthians 15:50). You cannot get to

---

2   Alexander Schmemann, *Our Father* (New York: St. Vladimir's Press, 2002), p. 55.

where you long to be if you start in the wrong place. You cannot feed your spirit with "flesh and blood." You will never "inherit the kingdom of God" with that which is "perishable." What you really long for is "substantive" bread.

When Jesus responds to the first temptation in the wilderness saying, "One does not live by bread alone, but by every word that comes from the mouth of God" (Matthew 4:4), he is implying that it is possible to be well fed with bread for the body and yet not be alive. When we feed only our bodies we are the living dead. Jesus said, "Life does not consist in the abundance of possessions" (Luke 12:15b). Nothing in the external physical realm can give you life. You may be alive, but you do not have "life" unless you are feeding on the "substantive" bread that Jesus instructed us to pray we might feed upon every day.

As with the earlier petitions in this prayer, we ourselves must be the answer to our own prayer. When we pray "give us this day our substantive bread," we must recognize that the prayer cannot be fulfilled by God alone. God can give bread, but bread is useless unless it is eaten, and God does not force-feed anyone. We are each responsible for taking advantage of the spiritual sustenance and nourishment which God provides.

God does provide. There is no famine. We are surrounded by "substantive" bread. Jesus said, "Take, eat, this is my body given for you." If we feel depleted we must ask ourselves whether we are feeding on the substantive bread that God provides, or whether we are still trying to find nourishment in junk food.

1. What is "substantive" bread? How have you experienced being fed with this kind of bread? What sources for this bread can you identify? What helps you to feed on this bread? What hinders you from feeding on this bread?

2. What forms of "junk food" are we tempted to consume in place of "real bread"? What is the attraction of "junk food"? What is the effect of "junk food" on our lives?

Notice your hunger. Identify those sources in your life which provide "substantive" bread. Find ways to strengthenthese sources of feeding in your life.

8

Food Without Fear

Matthew 6:11 (ii)

Give us today our daily bread.

If God wants to feed us with bread that has the power to nourish our innermost being, why do we so often experience ourselves as spiritually starving to death? Why do we feel depleted, rundown, overwhelmed, filled with anxieties, fears, uncertainties, and doubt? Why do we so often seem to be running on empty?

In John's gospel Jesus says, "I am the bread of life. Whoever comes to me will never be hungry, and whoever believes in me will never be thirsty" (John 6:35). Why is it so seldom that we experience *not* being hungry and thirsty? Why are we so often attacked by loneliness, fear, and worry?

Either Jesus is playing some strange game in telling us to pray for "substantive bread" that he knows God does not intend to give us. Or else God wants to give us this bread, but we are unwilling or unable to receive it.

Assuming that Jesus told us to pray "Give us today our daily bread" in the belief that God desires to answer the prayer, what might prevent us from eating the bread of life and experiencing the inner nourishment Jesus promises that God will provide?

To answer this question we need to reach back into ancient Hebrew tradition and remember the story of the Exodus. The Hebrew people had become slaves in Egypt, and after years of suffering in bondage, they were miraculously liberated and led by God out to the wilderness and into freedom. But when they got to the wilderness, things did not always go as smoothly as they might have hoped. There were no fast food outlets there, and they got hungry. The writer of Exodus tells us:

> The whole congregation of the Israelites complained against Moses and Aaron in the wilderness. The Israelites said to them, "If only we had died by the hand of the Lord in the land of Egypt, when we sat by the fleshpots and ate our fill of bread; for you have brought us out into this wilderness to kill this whole assembly with hunger" (16:2, 3).

It appears that Moses must have taken the problem to God, who replied:

> I am going to rain bread from heaven for you, and each day the people shall go out and gather a day's portion. In that way I will test them, whether they will follow my instruction or not. On the sixth day, when they prepare what they bring in, it will be twice as much as they gather on other days (16:4, 5).

God directs the people that each day they are to gather a day's portion, and on the sixth day they are to gather just enough for two days so that they don't have to go out to work on the Sabbath. The point is that God will provide enough for each day.

So what happened? When the food came they gathered all they needed for the day. Moses told them that at the end of each day there should be no leftovers. But "they did not listen to Moses. Some left part of it until morning" (16:20). You can imagine them saying, "Well, we should take a little extra just in case. What if there is no food tomorrow? Moses will never know." They were hoarding, saving just a little against a rainy day.

What happened to the saved bread? "It bred worms and became foul" (16:20).

They were being driven by fear, afraid that the food God had provided was going to run out. They viewed life in terms of scarcity, believing that the day would come when there would not be enough to go around. It's a very common way of thinking. But when we pray "Give us today our substantive bread," we are saying that there *is* enough to go around, not only today but also tomorrow.

I have heard stories of people who have experienced starvation. Even after their situation has changed and they have lived for months with an abundance of food, they still hoard leftovers and take more than they can eat. Their identities are still shaped by their experience of scarcity, and their fear prevents them from seeing the fullness that has been given to them. So it is with our experience of spiritual starvation.

In his book *Everything Belongs*, Richard Rohr says, "Some say that FEAR is merely an acronym for 'false evidence appearing real.'"[1] The reality to which Jesus points is that life is characterized by abundance. In all four gospels, Jesus feeds crowds, numbered variously at four or five thousand men plus women and children. After everyone has been fed and is filled, there are "twelve baskets full of broken pieces left over"

---

1   Richard Rohr, *Everything Belongs: The Gift of Contemplative Prayer* (New York: The Crossroad Publishing Company, 1999), p. 122.

(Matthew 14:20). It is only the "false evidence" that leads us to believe that there is not enough to go around and that we must fight hard for our own little piece of the pie.

Yet it is this very fight that prevents us from knowing the fullness which is Jesus. Grasping, grabbing, holding on, prevent us from receiving the real food of the living bread of Jesus Christ who feeds us with the substantive bread of his Spirit. Fear always works against fullness.

Fear is always fear of loss. Someone is going to take something from me. I am going to be left alone. I am going to lose my sense of self. My identity is threatened. We experience our world as deeply unstable, and in an unstable world we fear that something is going to be taken from us.

When we pray "Give us today our substantive bread," we are making a bold statement of faith that no one can take from us the only true food there is. Jesus is the bread for which our hearts long. Even when everything else is taken from us, we still have the bread of life living in us. There is nothing to fight for, nothing to hoard, nothing to protect, nothing to fear. We can rest in the nourishment given to us daily, the true bread that has come down from heaven to meet the deepest longings of our hearts.

1. How might we be tempted to hoard? What motivates hoarding? What do we hope to accomplish by hoarding? What is the impact of our hoarding?

2. What are we afraid of? What triggers our fears? Where do our fears come from? What causes us to continue in these fears?

Notice the feeling of fear rising up. Before responding from this fearful place, pause a moment and allow yourself to rest. Sink down into that deeper place that knows the fullness of God. When the fear has settled a little, choose to respond from this deeper place.

9

Uunconditional Forgiveness

Matthew 6:12 (i)

And forgive us our debts, as we also have forgiven our debtors.

The Lord's Prayer is a brilliant and carefully crafted piece of devotional spirituality. It begins with God. We then declare our intention to honour God. We move on to express our commitment to cooperate in the process of seeing God's kingdom come in the world and to seeing God's will done in our own lives. Then we pray that we may be sustained by God's presence in order to fulfill all that we have prayed for in the first section of the prayer. We ask, "Give us today our daily bread."

At this point the structure of the prayer becomes harder to follow. Why would the prayer for bread be followed immediately by the request for forgiveness? "Give us this day our daily bread. And forgive us our debts, as we also have forgiven our debtors."

When we say "Give us today our daily bread," we are asking

that we may be deeply nourished and sustained in our spiritual being. Forgiveness is the fundamental means by which we open ourselves to the nourishment that is the Spirit of Jesus.

One of the primary obstacles to receiving the bread with which God desires to nourish us is the presence of unforgiveness in our hearts. Without forgiveness we remain captive in the bitter little jails of our anger and resentment. If we cannot get free to experience forgiveness and extend it to others, we cannot receive the nourishment offered.

It is curious how little forgiveness really gets addressed in the Christian context. I don't think we really like forgiveness very much. I think it scares us.

Luke's gospel offers us the pre-eminent example of forgiveness in the New Testament. Jesus has just been subjected to a mockery of justice in a pretend trial that was only ever intended to condemn him to death. He has been mocked, scorned, beaten, spit upon, and then forced to walk through the streets of Jerusalem to the place of his execution. Then Luke tells us, "When they came to the place that is called The Skull, they crucified Jesus there with the criminals, one on his right and one on his left" (Luke 23:33).

The Roman soldiers took Jesus' already battered body, laid his back against rough beams of wood formed into a cross, nailed his hands in place, and raised up the cross before the crowds. Then hanging in agony on the cross, Jesus spoke to those below: "Father, forgive them; for they do not know what they are doing" (Luke 23:34). What an extraordinary thing to say at that moment!

Who is it that Jesus asks God to forgive? He can only mean those he sees before him — his tormentors. He sees the Roman general who gave the order for the hammer blows to start. He sees the soldiers who carried out the order and who now, as Jesus hangs dying, gamble for his last earthly belongings. He asks God to forgive them. He sees his own countrymen, the church officials of his day who pursued him relentlessly, mocking and ridiculing him because they said he claimed to be king of the Jews and they knew he was an impostor. He asks God to forgive them. He sees his own disciples, those who pledged to be faithful but in the end could not stand by in his hour of need. He sees Judas, who betrayed him, and Peter, who denied him. He asks God to forgive them. And he sees all those passing by who ignored him and asks God to forgive them. Jesus gathers them all into the arms of his loving embrace and prays God to forgive and forgive and forgive.

Jesus sees you and me too, and he asks God to forgive us. Why does Jesus ask God to forgive us all? Have we seen the error of our ways, repented, and pleaded for God's forgiveness? Have we turned our lives around and started to walk in the light of God's truth? No.

In the crucifixion story there is only one person who shows any sign of remorse. One of the criminals crucified with Jesus turned and asked, "Jesus, remember me when you come into your kingdom" (Luke 23:42). Yet Jesus' prayer for forgiveness embraces everyone. It comes before any of us one have seen the error of our ways, before we have renounced violence, got our act together, or reformed. Jesus' prayer for forgiveness is addressed to God on behalf of those of us who are still caught in the sin and confusion of our divided lives.

Forgiveness by its very nature comes before repentance, before it is even sought. That is why we don't like to think about forgiveness and why it scares us. It wipes out all categories of right and wrong.

Forgiveness does not presume to judge. Judgment tries to create a tidy world in which we know who is good and who is bad. Judgment believes that we can understand how life works. Jesus cuts across all superficial judgments and says simply, "Father, forgive them, for they do not know what they are doing." It is not that they are bad; it is only that they are trapped in an illusion.

People do bad things not because they are evil, but because they do not see clearly. They look for life in all the wrong places. And when we look for life in the wrong places, the fruit of our lives is always violence. Forgiveness breaks the cycle of violence by acknowledging that we cannot sit in judgment on anyone. Only God sees into the human heart, and having seen, God forgives.

If we are going to forgive the way Jesus forgave, we will not wait for others to see how wrong they have been. We will not wait for them to see the error of their ways and to know that we were right all along. We forgive them as they continue to hammer the nails into our hands. We forgive them as they continue to utter threats and to mock and ridicule us. We forgive them in the midst of our own pain, before anything is resolved or worked out.

The forgiveness Jesus offers is not the forgiveness that comes from a position of superiority or power. Instead, it is offered to us in our weakness, where we are vulnerable and suffering.

This is the only kind of forgiveness that can truly set us free from the prisons of our own suffering. It expects nothing in return, comes with no strings attached. It does not demand that conditions be fulfilled before it is offered. It says, "You can hurt me. You can misuse me. You can take advantage of me. But you can not ever take from me the freedom to forgive you for the wrong that I experience." This is the extraordinary dignity Jesus modelled for us on the cross. It is the grace we claim from God when we pray "forgive us our debts." And it is the power we seek from God when we add, "as we also have forgiven our debtors."

1. How do we understand forgiveness? How does the world understand forgiveness? In what ways might our understanding of forgiveness be challenged by the picture of forgiveness we find in Jesus?

2. Why is forgiveness so difficult? What can I do that might help make forgiveness a more natural response in my life?

Identify a hurt in your life, a person or situation that causes you pain. See how this situation has emerged from the hurt in the other person's life or in your own life. Allow your heart to soften towards that person or yourself. Open and embrace the situation.

10

Forgiveness Is Letting Go

Matthew 6:12 (ii)

Forgive us our debts, as we also forgive our debtors.

Jesus instructs us to pray, "Forgive us our debts, as we also forgive our debtors." I am using the words "debts" and "debtors" rather than the more familiar "trespasses" and "those who trespass against us," or "sins" and "those who sin against us."

The Greek in Matthew's gospel refers to literal debts, and it means exactly what we think it means: it has clear financial overtones. The financial implications of the word teach us something important about the nature of forgiveness.

As a family we try to live pretty much within our means financially. There are times when it seems that the inflow of cash risks falling a little bit behind the outflow of cash; but mostly they balance, and we have never really been in debt.

Some time ago on one of those occasions when the outflow seemed to be faster than the inflow, I wasn't sure that I could cover my full credit card payment on the due date. I decided to pay half the bill on the due date and the other half immediately after payday, which was only three days after the payment was due. After all, surely the interest on half the bill for three days could not be very high. How little I knew and how much I learned when the next bill arrived with a large interest payment due. I immediately called the 1-800 number to inform my friendly customer service agent that a terrible mistake had been made. "I cannot believe that this interest charge represents three days' interest on half my bill."

"Well sir," the nice man informed me, "you see, as soon as you are a day late on any portion of your total payment you are charged interest on the entire bill for the full month represented by that bill."

There was a long, long pause on my end of the phone. Then just before the nice man in faraway customer-service-land called 911 to say he had a customer on the line who was in coronary arrest, I managed to say faintly, "Oh, I don't think I had understood that that is how it works."

This should be the end of the story, but even in credit-card-land, there is grace for stupidity. The customer service man said, "Well sir, I will take off the interest charge on your next bill." My debt was gone, forgiven, wiped out. The agent had released me from it. I was free again from the grip of debt.

Then I understood what forgiveness is. Forgiveness is letting go. When we let someone go, we release them from our grip. We no longer demand something of them. We no longer require that they satisfy our needs, desires, or wishes. We unbind them from the prison of our expectations. Forgiveness puts freedom in the place of bondage.

Forgiveness does not keep a record of wrongs. It does not demand justice, retribution, or balance. Instead, it overturns the tables of the money changers in the temple who weigh and measure everything by its dollar value.

When we ask God to forgive us our debts, we are asking to join the ranks of those who have all the wrongs they have ever done wiped out. We are asking God for freedom from what we owe and have not paid. It follows that those who have experienced true freedom can only extend the same generous, open, gracious gift of freedom to all those with whom they have contact.

The answer to violence is not more violence. The answer to the psychic pain of the wrongs that have been done to us is not to cling to our rights and shoulder our bitterness as a badge of our longsuffering identity. The only answer to the violence and chaos that mars our world is for someone to choose to let go. Someone has to be the first to release the one by whom they feel they have been wronged. Someone has to have the courage to break the cycle of violence and retribution.

On the cross, Jesus made that break and pointed the way forward through the morass of suffering that characterizes so much of the human community. Jesus pointed the way past the pain towards the possibility of new life and peace.

In his reflections on the terrible events of 11 September 2001, Archbishop Rowan Williams tells the story of being called by a Welsh news reporter on 12 September. The reporter began the conversation in Welsh, and Williams had to decide whether to respond in Welsh or switch the conversation to English. He points out that the language in which we choose to respond is the language in which the conversation will continue.[1]

On the cross Jesus chose a radically different language of response. When we forgive, we change the discourse from the language of violence and retribution to the language of love.

---

1   Rowan Williams, *Writing in the Dust: After September 11* (Grand Rapids: William B. Eerdmans, 2002), p. 15.

The challenge for those of us who pray this prayer and follow the one who was raised through death, is to take up the language of forgiveness and practice the same radical release that Jesus showed on the cross.

1. How might we attempt to bind other people? What do we feel like when we encounter someone else's attempts to bind us? What does this mutual binding look like in human community?

2. How do we see the language of violence at work in the world, in our own lives, in the church? What are the effects of this language?

Notice when you become aware of the language of violence in your environment. Try to find a way that your language of response can change the direction and tone of the discourse.

11

The Dance of Forgiveness

Matthew 6:12 (iii)

Forgive us our debts as we also forgive our debtors.

The petition "forgive us our debts as we also forgive our debtors" is the only place in the Lord's Prayer where Jesus follows the prayer with a word of explanation.

In Matthew's gospel, after the Lord's Prayer is completed, Jesus goes on to say, "For if you forgive others their trespasses, your heavenly Father will also forgive you, but if you do not forgive others their trespasses, neither will your Father forgive your trespasses" (Matthew 6:14). In the *New Revised Standard Version*, the entire Lord's Prayer is made up of only 52 words. This explanatory note to verse 12 consists of 30 words. Jesus obviously felt that "forgive us our debts, as we also have forgiven our debtors" was an important part of the prayer.

We need to deal carefully with verse 12 and the explanatory verses 14 and 15, where Jesus seems to be presenting a principle of reciprocity. He seems to suggest that the way we are able to forgive shapes the way we will be able to be forgiven.

This idea of reciprocity is not unique to Jesus in the Christian Scriptures. Paul says, "You reap whatever you sow" (Galatians 6:7), and "The one who sows sparingly will also reap sparingly, and the one who sows bountifully will also reap bountiful" (2 Corinthians 9:6).

What are we to make of this idea of reciprocity in our relationship with God? It is not a formula by which we can control God, as if we could say to God, "I will do this and then you must do that." God cannot be controlled. Jesus too is unpredictable. No one is in charge of him except the divine Source from which he came.

This prayer is not a recipe to put us in charge of God, and the Christian faith is not a contractual agreement with God. It is a relationship of grace, not a relationship of law. As we saw in this sectin of the book, God's forgiveness precedes even our awareness of our need to be forgiven.

What Jesus is offering in the Lord's prayer is not a prescription for spiritual control, but simply a statement of spiritual reality. If we do not forgive others, our hearts cannot open to receive the forgiveness that God has already offered to us. In our earlier discussion of forgiveness, we saw that forgiveness is letting go. Letting go means opening and embracing. Those who cannot open, cannot receive. You can try all you want to give me love, forgiveness, and acceptance, but if I am closed to you, resisting your efforts, I cannot receive your love.

Love and forgiveness move together in an intimate dance. I am no dancer, but I think that when a couple are attempting to dance in an intimate embrace with one another, the dance is going to be extremely difficult if one partner is resisting the other. In order to dance in harmony, both partners must open to each other and surrender themselves to the music. They must hear the rhythm of the orchestra and be willing to flow with the sound.

Resistance kills the dance. The spiritual teacher Eckhart

Tolle says, "inner resistance cuts you off from other people, from yourself, from the world around."[1] Ultimately resistance cuts us off from God. It causes God's freely offered forgiveness to fall stillborn on the floor at our feet.

We create what we are. If we are bound, pinched, and tight, we create bounded-ness, pinched-ness, and tightness wherever we go. If we are free, open, relaxed, and at peace, we will create freedom, openness, relaxation, and peace wherever we go. We can only receive from God what we are open to receiving. The sign of being open to receive is the ability to pass on what has been received.

God offers and offers and offers. The moment I decide to offer, I am opened to be able to receive the grace and the mercy and the welcome that God constantly extends towards me. It is not that I am controlling God. It is simply that I cannot receive that to which I am closed.

Nor can I ask from God what I am not able to pass on, because I cannot receive from God what I am not able to share. If I come to you with my arms crossed over my chest and my face set in a stern grimace and say to you, "Give me a hug," you are unlikely to fulfill my request. Everything in my body is resisting the hug that I am asking for.

When we pray "forgive us our debts, as we also have forgiven our debtors," we are asking for the openness to receive the very thing for which we ask. We are saying to God, "Open us to you as we have opened ourselves to others, even those who have hurt us." We are committing ourselves to lay down our bitterness, our resentment. We are surrendering any

---

1   Eckhart Tolle, *The Power of Now: A Guide To Spiritual Enlightenment* (Vancouver, B.C.: Namaste Publishing, 1997), p. 113.

unforgiveness that may lurk in the dark corners of our hearts. We are opening ourselves to fully embrace the presence of God in our lives. And as we embrace God, we are embracing all of God's creatures. Any place of closure in our hearts will close that little bit of our being to God's presence.

So if God seems absent, we need to look carefully within our own heart and ask ourselves about the state of our forgiveness. What might there be in life that we are rejecting and closing ourselves to?

Every closure to anything in all of God's Creation is a closure to God. Any resistance to life as it is, is a resistance to God. To pray the Lord's Prayer and open to receive the presence of the living God is to let go of anything that might hinder God's work and know the presence of God filling your being with forgiving love.

———

1. What causes us to brace against life? What are the sources of resistance? How does resistance translate into action in our lives?

2. What reality are the choices, decisions, and attitudes of our lives creating?

Watch any resistance in yourself. Observe where you carry this resistance in your body. Try to relax that part of your body and allow your resistance to soften.

12

Deliverance from Suffering

Matthew 6:13 (i)

Lead us not into temptation, but deliver us from evil.

Matthew 6:13 is one of the most difficult and puzzling verses in all of Scripture. The problem falls in the first half of the verse where Jesus instructs us to pray, "lead us not into temptation." God does not lead people into temptation. The writer of the Letter of James says, "No one when tempted, should say, 'I am being tempted by God,' for God cannot be tempted with evil, and he himself tempts no one" (James 1:13). Immediately after his baptism when Jesus "was led up by the Spirit into the wilderness to be tempted by the devil" (Matthew 4:1), the temptations did not come from God but from "the devil."

Temptation is an inevitable part of the human condition. We are surrounded by it for our entire lives. Even Jesus faced temptation up to his dying hour. So "lead us not into temptation" seems to be a ridiculous prayer.

Scholars have tried to translate their way out of the difficulty. The Canadian Anglican *Book of Alternative Services* escapes the problem by translating verse 13 to read "Save us from the time of trial." This makes sense because we all know there are times when we need to be delivered from trial. In the *BAS* translation the prayer expresses our hope that we may not be overcome by those temptations that are an inevitable part of life.

Unfortunately, however, this does not seem to be what Matthew 6:13 actually means. The Greek word that the *BAS* has translated as "save us" is *eisphero*, which means "bring in, carry in, or lead." Furthermore, in Greek the request is negative; it is asking God *not* to do something.

The *Good News Bible* tries to get around the problem by having Jesus instruct us to pray "Do not bring us to hard testing." But surely this is not a prayer Jesus would ever ask us to pray. The Bible teaches consistently that testing is good for us. James writes, "My brothers and sisters, whenever you face trials of any kind, consider it nothing but joy, because you know that the testing of your faith produces endurance" (James 1:2, 3).

Jesus placed at the heart of our faith the awareness that life in this world will always involve some measure of strife, struggle, disharmony, and discomfort. This is reality. As Christians we should not be surprised when we find ourselves wrestling with the realities of life in a broken, imperfect world.

Our problem arises when we think that something unusual is happening to us when we face suffering. We tend to think that we are the first or only person in the world who has ever had to wrestle with whatever our problems are. But Paul reminds us, "No testing has overtaken you that is not common to everyone. God is faithful, and he will not let you be tested beyond your strength, but with the testing he will also provide the way out so that you may be able to endure it" (I Corinthians 10:13).

The desert mystics of Egypt also knew the truth: "Abba Anthony said to Abba Poemen, 'This is the great work of a man: always to take the blame for his own sins before God and to expect temptation to his last breath.'" But they also knew that the struggle is not the problem; the problem is giving up. Another desert saying tells us, "Abraham said, 'It is not new to fall, my daughter; what is wrong is to lie down when you have fallen ... sin is only part of being human.'"

Life is a process of falling down and getting up, falling down and getting up, falling down and getting up, over and over and over.

But the promise of the Lord's Prayer is the same promise that Paul gives us: "God is faithful, and he will not let you be tested beyond your strength, but with the testing he will also provide the way out so that you may be able to endure it" (I Corinthians 10:13). It is easy, in the midst of trials and temptations, to forget God's faithfulness. That is why we need to pray, over and over again "deliver us from evil." These words affirm the reality of deliverance. We may not see how God's deliverance is coming, but God is always faithful and deliverance is always available. We need only to ask to see more clearly how it is that God has answered our prayer and provided deliverance in the midst of our struggle and our trial.

The second half of the verse, "deliver us from evil," clearly recognizes that there are going to be times when we are in need of deliverance from evil — times when difficult things afflict us, when we suffer, when we feel that we cannot endure, when we do not know how we are going to get through it all. Deliverance, when it comes, may not always look exactly as we had hoped it might. But if we have eyes to see and ears to hear, it is always there.

So where does this leave us in dealing with the prayer "lead us not into temptation?" We cannot translate our way out of the problem. We cannot interpret it in a way that makes the first half of the prayer contradict the second half. So we will have to wrestle with how we are to understand it.

This wrestling itself may be part of the answer. There are no easy answers in the face of human suffering. The very process of having to stay open in the face of our inability to fully understand is part of the message of biblical sayings whose meaning is not immediately obvious. The Bible does not provide easy, tidy answers to difficult, painful questions. We need to let the questions do their work in our hearts, creating a more wide open space within our spirits to embrace the struggles and uncertainties of the human condition.

The Desert Fathers said, "Sit in your cell and your cell will teach you everything." Stay with your struggle. Sit with the difficulties, doubts, and confusion. Do not rush too quickly to an easy resolution for the tension of not knowing. The deepest conundrums of the human condition are chisels working on the granite block of our lives. The chisel of suffering and confusion chip away at the hard exterior, seeking to release the inner beauty that is the truth of our human condition.

1. What are some of the most common responses we encounter in reaction to human suffering? How does it feel to acknowledge the reality and the inevitability of human suffering and struggle?

2. How do we experience deliverance in the midst of suffering and struggle? What does deliverance look like? Where does it most commonly come from? What can we do to cooperate with the process of deliverance?

When you find yourself in the midst of a difficult situation avoid the temptation to give in to despair. Keep an open expectant attitude watching for the deliverance that is promised.

13

Toying with Temptation

Matthew 6:13 (ii)

Lead us not into temptation, but deliver us from evil.

Since many commentators simply ignore the problems in the petition, "lead us not into temptation," I feel bold in offering my own slightly odd reading of this verse. I think Jesus asks us to pray this prayer not because God needs to hear it, but because we need to pray it.

Think for a moment about the structure of the Lord's Prayer. In the petition immediately preceding the request that we not be led into temptation Jesus tells us to pray "forgive us our debts, as we forgive our debtors." This petition deals with the past. Forgiveness wipes out our past. Those who are forgiven and who extend forgiveness to others enter every situation in life with a clean slate. Those who regularly practice forgiveness have no regrets or resentments to continue lugging around.

So having dealt with the past in verse 12, Jesus directs our attention to the future in verse 13 where we think about where our lives may be headed. And in the first half of verse 13 we are being asked to express our desire to stay away from tempting situations.

What if we prayed the opposite: "God, lead us into temptation"? That may sound ludicrous, but there are times when we would like to sniff around the edges of some little unpleasantness we know is contrary to God's best purpose for our lives.

Have you ever found yourself listening to a conversation in which something less than edifying was being shared? Did you edge a little closer, to hear the juicy details? Have you ever gone to the mall knowing your credit card is already struggling under the burden of interest bearing debt you have accumulated and that you really cannot afford to purchase another thing. So you say, "Oh, I will just go window shopping." Are you not praying, "God lead me into temptation?"

The prayer "forgive us our debts as we forgive our debtors" expresses again the principle we have seen throughout this prayer, that to some extent we get from life what we put into life. If we play with temptation, we find more temptation springing up. Life will produce more and more tempting situations. In a sense God is leading us into temptation, by allowing life to produce circumstances that we have helped to create. If we really want temptation, God will let us have it.

Jesus wants us to refresh our commitment to staying away from situations that lead us to those harmful things we often want for ourselves. He knows that sin begins with the little mind games we play. It begins when we decide we will put ourselves in the way of temptation or when we start to compromise.

To pray "lead us not into temptation" is to pray, "keep me from compromise; keep me focused on your will and your best purpose for my life." In this final petition of the Lord's Prayer, we are confessing to God that all those false things we have chased can never truly satisfy us. We are affirming our faith that God alone satisfies the deepest longings of our hearts. We are expressing our desire to chart the course of our lives by the perfect will of God. This is a prayer that will serve us well throughout our entire lives.

This final petition sums up the entire prayer. The whole prayer has been about the state of our inner lives. In the Lord's Prayer Jesus invites us to take responsibility for our own inner lives. He invites us to examine our priorities, to ask ourselves what things are really important to us and how our priorities are reflected in our daily lives.

We have affirmed in this prayer that God is present throughout all of life. We have expressed our desire that God's will may be done throughout the world and in our own individual lives. We have recognized that sustenance for life comes from God alone and that those who know God's will live in relationships of forgiveness with all people. Now, finally, we reaffirm our conviction that God alone is the only priority in our lives.

For Jesus, God is not the first in a long list of life's priorities; God is the only priority. God's claims upon our lives are absolute for the simple reason that God is the centre around which everything else revolves. There is no competition. The only way to a truly healthy spiritual life is to abandon every other claim upon our allegiance. God needs to be the shape to which everything else conforms. The way we spend our money, our time, our energy, our conversation, all need to take shape around the single reality of God's presence at the heart of our lives and at the centre of the universe. Anything less than this is less than God desires for us.

This does not mean we all have to move to the desert to live a life of solitude and prayer, but it does mean that the external dimensions of life on which we spend so much time and energy are always of secondary importance. To pray "lead us not into temptation" is to ask God to keep us from frittering away our lives on things that are not central to who we truly are as human beings. We are asking God to keep us in tune with God's will and in tune with our true nature. And we are asking God to protect us from those things that will lead us into the evil from which we will then need to be delivered.

This whole prayer tells us who we truly are as human beings created in the image of God. Anything that does not come from this prayer is something less than God desires for us. The Lord's Prayer is the way to freedom and life for those who pray it and follow its directions.

1. How might you be praying "lead me into temptation"? What is it about the temptations that you want to be led into that makes them so compelling?

2. What might it mean to make God the only priority around which everything else in our entire lives would take shape and to which every dimension of our lives would conform?

When you experience temptation, ask yourself how much you are cooperating in giving this temptation power in your life. Recall the deeper commitment of your heart to keeping God at the centre and allowing everything else to take shape around the deep invisible reality of God's love.

Path Books

A LIGHT TO MY PATH

We hope that you have enjoyed reading this Path Book. For more information about Path Books, please visit our website at **www.pathbooks.com**. If you have comments or suggestions about Path Books, please write us at publisher@pathbooks.com.

Other Path Books

Sacred Simplicities: Seeing the Miracles in Our Lives by Lori Knutson. In these engaging, two-page stories, Knutson shares her experience of the divine in the everyday, helping us to see glimpses of God where we least expect them. Enrichment for time at home or while travelling, meditations with nature, or sermon illustrations.
1-55126-419-6 $18.95

Oceans of Grief and Healing Waters: A Story of Loss and Recovery by Marian Jean Haggerty. With courageous candour and strength, Marian Haggerty tells the story of her journey toward healing from grief, after the death of a loved one. This book can be a wonderful companion for those who are alone and grieving, helping them to understand that they do not journey by themselves.
1-55126-396-3 $16.95

Struggling with Forgiveness: Stories from People and Communities by David Self. These powerful firsthand stories reflect the tremendous range of our experience of conflict and forgiveness: in families, at work, between individuals, within whole societies. They reveal how forgiveness can break the cycle of bitterness, revenge, and violence. There is such possibility for release and healing.
1-55126-395-5 $19.95

From Fear to Freedom: Abused Wives Find Hope and Healing by Sheila A. Rogers. This book recounts the spiritual journey of five women as they move from childhood into abusive marriages, and then out into self-realization and freedom. The women share their thoughts and feelings about thenmselves, their abusers, and God. The book offers practical advice for those who have experienced abuse, and for their friends and family.
1-55126-358-0 $19.95

Practical Prayer: Making Space for God in Everyday Life by Anne Tanner. A richly textured presentation of the history, practices, and implications of Christian prayer and meditation to help people live a rewarding life in a stressful world.
1-55126-321-1 $18.95
Meditation CD: 1-55126-348-3 $18.95
Audio cassette: 1-55126-349-1 $16.95
Leader's Guide: 1-55126-347-5 $18.95

Healing Through Prayer: Health Practitioners Tell the Story by Larry Dossey, Herbert Benson, John Polkinghorne, and Others. Prayer is powerful. In this unique book and video, doctors and patients quote scientific surveys and relate personal experiences of healing through prayer. They provide new conviction to people of faith, and new hope to those seeking healing. *1-55126-229-0, 168 pages, paper $18.95*
The Power Within, one-hour video
1-55126-234-7, $29.95

God with Us: The Companionship of Jesus in the Challenges of Life by Herbert O'Driscoll. In thirty-three perceptive meditations, Herbert O'Driscoll considers the challenges of being human, searches key events in the life of Jesus, and discovers new vitality and guidance for our living. He shows us how the healing wisdom and power of Jesus' life can transform our own lives today.
1-55126-359-9 $18.95

Available from your local bookstore or
Anglican Book Centre, phone 1-800-268-1168
or write 80 Hayden Street, Toronto, ON M4Y 3G2.